W9-DCC-345

T H E
HISTORY HIGHWAY
A Guide To Internet Resources

T H E
HISTORY HIGHWAY

A Guide To Internet Resources

DENNIS A. TRINKLE
DOROTHY AUCHTER
SCOTT A. MERRIMAN
TODD E. LARSON

M.E. Sharpe
Armonk, New York
London, England

Library of Congress Cataloging-in-Publication Data

The history highway : a guide to Internet resources /
Dennis A. Trinkle . . . [et al.].
p.   cm.
Includes bibliographical references and index.
ISBN 0–7656–0010–2 (hc : alk. paper). —
ISBN 0–7656–0011–0 (pbk. : alk. paper)
1. History—Computer network resources.
2. Internet (Computer network)
I. Trinkle, Dennis A., 1968– .
D16.255.C65H58
1996
025.06′9—dc20
96–42240
CIP

Printed in the United States of America

The paper used in this publication meets the minimum requirements of
American National Standard for Information Sciences—
Permanence of Paper for Printed Library Materials,
ANSI Z 39.48-1984.

BM (c)   10   9   8   7   6   5   4   3   2   1
BM (p)   10   9   8   7   6   5   4   3   2   1

Contents

Acknowledgments

The only debts that are pleasant to recall are those acquired in long, collaborative projects such as *The History Highway*. We would like to recognize all those who helped make this work possible.

Dennis A. Trinkle would like to thank Dorothy Auchter, Scott Merriman, and Todd Larson for making this collaborative effort a joy. I would also like to acknowledge those teachers and professors who provided their advice, encouragement, and support during the various stages of my education. My sincere thanks to John Baughman, John Dittmer, Frank Kafker, Gene Lewis, John Brackett, Barbara Ramusack, and Maura O'Connor; their lessons and examples live in this work. The contents of the book were also shaped through many conversations with colleagues in history whom I am fortunate to count as friends: Joseph Fultz, Don McArthur, Sean Marcum, Peggy Hill, Ian Binnington, and Thomas Neville. This book would never have been written without material support from the University of Cincinnati and the Charles Taft Fund. It would also never have been completed without the love and encouragement of my family and friends. My mother, wife, brother, and brother-in-law all read parts of the book in manuscript, offering suggestions above and beyond the call of family. For them I offer a special thanks.

Dorothy Auchter would like to thank Jane and John Auchter for their help in revising this manuscript. Their support and encouragement in this project, as in so many other areas, has been a blessing.

Scott A. Merriman wishes to acknowledge those who have helped him with this venture and in the larger journey of life. I would like to thank Dennis Trinkle for his paramount assistance. For serving as colleagues and examples, I would like to recognize Michael Adams and

James Westheider. Daniel Beaver, Roger Daniels, and David Sterling deserve special thanks as mentors and for demonstrating what a professor and scholar is supposed to be. In my larger travels, I have been ably assisted by many people, and I would be remiss if I did not thank them here. I am truly grateful for my continuing friendships with Joan Blaylock, Rowly Brucken, Randal Horobik, Jen McGee, Thomas Neville, Paul Wexler, and Andrew Wilson. I am grateful to my family for their perpetual support. Finally, for all those who supported me, but who are not specifically mentioned, thanks!

Todd E. Larson would like to thank Marc T. Hanger of Loyola University for sharing his ideas during the formative stages of this project back in 1993. A number of people have since offered cogent advice and support. They include, but are not limited to, Professors Maura O'Connor and Frank Kafker of the University of Cincinnati's history department; the faculty of the department of history at the University of Illinois at Urbana-Champaign, especially Professors Orville Vernon Burton, Charles Stewart, Elizabeth Pleck, and my adviser, Walter Arnstein; David Herr of NCSA; Ian Binnington; Joan B. Blaylock; and my wife, Heidi J. Larson. A sincere thanks to all for their help and support.

Introduction

Welcome to the information superhighway. The Internet is a tremendously exciting place these days. The amount and variety of information available is truly staggering. Unfortunately, trying to jump in and sample the Internet is like trying to sip water from a fire hose. The information superhighway can be information overload at its worst, and to first-time users it is often more intimidating than exciting. For anyone interested in history, however, the Internet simply cannot be ignored. The resources are too rich and valuable. Students can find complete texts of thousands of books and hundreds of sites dedicated to historical topics. Publishers can advertise their wares, and professors can find enormous databases devoted to teaching suggestions, on-line versions of historical journals, and active scholarly discussions on a wide variety of research topics. The Internet is quite simply the most revolutionary storehouse of human knowledge in history.

For most of us, however, whether we are students, professors, librarians, editors, or just lovers of history, there are not enough hours in our already busy days to go chasing information down an infinite number of alleyways, no matter how useful or interesting that information might be. This is especially true for those of us who have never logged on to a computer network or who have only a basic acquaintance with the Internet. The aim of this book is to provide a general introduction to the skills and tools necessary to navigate the information superhighway and to offer detailed information about the thousands of resources that are out there and how to find them.

Chapter 1 is a short primer for those with little or no experience using the Internet. It discusses what is out there and what you can do with it. It explains how to gain access to the Internet and outlines what types of software are necessary. There is also an important section on the manners and rules that govern the Internet—"Netiquette," as seasoned users call it.

Chapter 2 is the heart of the book. It directs readers to thousands of sites that will appeal to anyone interested in history. There are collections of historical documents, research library catalogs, paintings depicting the French Enlightenment, memoirs written by Benjamin Franklin, and journals such as *American Historical Review.* Of course, since the Internet is growing and changing every day, no book can hope to list every site. A careful effort has been made, however, to list those sites that are of the highest quality and contain the most useful information. *The History Highway* also has its own Internet site at http://www.uc.edu/www/history/highway.html which will list any address changes as they occur and any new sites as they come along. *The History Highway* will therefore serve as an evolving road map as you travel down the Internet thoroughfares. Bon voyage!

THE
HISTORY HIGHWAY
A Guide To Internet Resources

Chapter One

Getting Started

History of the Internet

Since this book is directed at people interested in history, it seems sensible to begin with a brief history of the Internet itself. Ironically, the Net began as the polar opposite of the publicly accessible network it has become. The project was initiated by the Advanced Research Projects Division (ARPA) of the Department of Defense in 1969 as a way to link universities, defense contractors, and military command centers so that communications would not be severed in case of nuclear attack. ARPANET, as it was labeled, was running by 1970, allowing military researchers to share information, and military scientists to explore computer command controls. The network grew quickly, adding the ability to handle electronic mail, to transfer data files, and to maintain group mailing lists.

In the early 1970s, it became clear to the initial developers of the ARPANET that the system was already stretching past its cold war origins. Nonmilitary research institutions were developing competing networks of communication, more and more users were going on-line, and new languages were being introduced, which made communication difficult or impossible between networks. To resolve this problem, the Defense Advanced Project Agency (which had replaced ARPA) launched the Internetting Project in 1973. The aim was to create a uniform communications language (a protocol) that would allow the hundreds of networks being formed to communicate and function as a single meganetwork. In an amazing display of scientific prowess comparable to the Apollo Program, this crucial

3

step in the development of the information superhighway was accomplished in a single year when Robert Kahn and Vinton G. Cerf introduced the Transmission Control Protocol/Internet Protocol (TCP/IP). This protocol (as the rules governing a computer language are termed) made possible the connection of all the various networks and computers then in existence and set the stage for the enormous expansion of the Internet.

Over the next decade, the Department of Defense realized the significance and potential of the Internet, and nonmilitary organizations were gradually allowed to link with the ARPANET. Shortly after that, commercial providers like CompuServe began making the Internet accessible to those not connected to a university or research institution. The potential for profiting from the Internet fueled dramatic improvements in speed and ease of use.

The most significant step toward simplicity of use came with the introduction of the World Wide Web (WWW), which allows interactive graphics and audio to be accessed through the Internet. The World Wide Web was the brainchild of Tim Berners-Lee of the European Laboratory for Particle Physics, who created a computer language called "hypertext" that made possible the interactive exchange of text and graphic images and allowed almost instantaneous connection (linking) to any item on the Internet. Berners-Lee was actually developing this revolutionary language as the Internet was expanding in the 1970s and 1980s, but it was only with the introduction of an easy-to-use Web browser (as the software for interacting with the Web is called) that the Web became widely accessible to the average person. That first browser—Mosaic—was made available to the public by the National Center for Supercomputing Applications at the University of Illinois, Urbana-Champaign, in 1991.

Today, there are many software packages competing with Mosaic and access to the Internet can be purchased through thousands of local providers. One need no longer be a military researcher or work at a university to "surf the Net." Best-guess estimates suggest there are probably 25 million to 30 million users logging onto the Internet from the United States alone. Tens of thousands of networks now are connected by TCP/IP, and the Internet forms a vast communication system that can legitimately be called an information superhighway. The best part is that you do not need a license to cruise this electronic autobahn.

Uses of the Internet

This section of chapter 1 will explain the most useful features of the Internet and give a broad sense of what is possible. It will discuss sending and receiving e-mail, reading and posting messages to Usenet newsgroups and discussion lists, logging on to remote computers with Telnet, transferring files using the File Transfer Protocol, and browsing the World Wide Web. The next section will discuss in greater detail the software packages that perform these tasks and explain exactly how to get on-line.

Sending and Receiving E-Mail

E-mail (electronic mail) is the most popular feature of the Internet. It offers almost instantaneous communication with people all over the world. E-mail functions like the U.S. Postal Service, allowing users to send and receive messages or computer files. Rather than taking days or weeks to reach their destination, however, e-mail messages arrive in minutes. A professor in Indianapolis, Indiana, can correspond with a student in Delhi, India, in the blink of an eye. A publisher, editor, and author can exchange drafts of a history book they are preparing with no delay. And e-mail does not involve the high costs of international postage, fax charges, or long-distance telephone premiums. E-mail is always part of the basic service arrangement provided with Internet access, and it is quite easy to use with the software packages discussed later.

A Note on E-Mail Addresses

E-mail addresses are very similar to postal addresses. Like a postal address, an e-mail address provides specific information about where the message is to be sent along the Internet. For example, a friend's address might be something like
TBinnington@edenvax.indiana.edu
If you look at the end of the address, you will notice the .edu suffix.

This means the e-mail message is going to an educational institution. In this case, it is Indiana University, as the second item indicates. Edenvax shows that the message is traveling along the Net to someone on a Vax computer designated as Eden at Indiana University. Finally, the address reveals that the recipient is your friend Todd Binnington (TBinnington). This is just like providing the name, street address, city, state, and zip code on regular mail.

The names that individual institutions choose for their Internet address vary widely, but to help make e-mail addresses a little easier to understand, all addresses in the United States are broken down into the computer equivalent of zip codes. We already noted the .edu in the above message indicated the recipient's account was at an educational institution. There are six such three-letter designations that provide a clue as to where your e-mail is going or coming from. They are:

Category	Meaning
• Com	Commercial organizations
• Edu	Educational institutions
• Gov	Government organizations (nonmilitary)
• Mil	Military institutions
• Net	Network service providers
• Org	Miscellaneous providers

These designations do not apply to e-mail addresses for accounts located outside the United States, but an equally simple system exists for identifying foreign messages. All mail going to or coming from foreign accounts ends with a two-letter country code. If you have a colleague in France, you might receive an e-mail message ending with .fr. You may receive an e-mail message from an editor in Canada ending in .ca. Or, if you met a historian with similar interests on that last trip through Tanzania, you might soon receive mail ending with .tz.

A Note on E-Mail Security

Because sending e-mail is so similar to sending a letter by postal service, many people forget that there is a major difference—federal laws discourage anyone from looking at (or intercepting) your mail, and sealed packaging provides a fairly reliable way to detect tampering. Unfortunately, e-mail is not protected in the same ways. As your electronic message passes through the Internet, it can be read, intercepted, and altered by many individuals.

Some security measures have been developed to protect e-mail just as an envelope secures letters. The latest versions of many programs that process e-mail now include the ability to encrypt messages. Encryption converts your e-mail into a complex code which must be deciphered by an e-mail program or Web browser that is designed to convert the encoded message back into regular text. The latest versions of Netscape, Mosaic, Eudora, and Pegasus include the ability to code and decode encrypted e-mail, but no e-mail program automatically converts a message into a secured code. If you want your messages or files encrypted, you will have to follow the directions provided with your e-mail package for doing it. If you purchase products and services over the Internet, you will also want to be certain that your account or credit card numbers are insured by some sort of encryption.

Reading and Posting Messages on Usenet Newsgroups

For anyone interested in history, Usenet newsgroups are another rewarding feature of the Internet. They are the electronic equivalent of the old New England town meetings in which anyone could pose a question or make an observation and others could respond to it. At present, there are nearly ten thousand newsgroups dedicated to thousands of different topics, and many of these relate to history. Each is regulated by a moderator who, like the editor of a newspaper, sets the quality and tone of the posts. There are groups that regularly discuss the Holocaust, the American Revolution, historical publishing, library concerns, and cartography, just to mention a few areas.

The software that allows one to easily locate and participate in these newsgroups will be discussed later. Before passing on to the next topic, however, there are several clues to determining the content and nature of groups that will help down the road. Like e-mail addresses, the addresses of newsgroups provide some insight into the nature of the group. Take the newsgroup

alt.civilwar

This address indicates that the group discusses the alternative topic— the Civil War. Each newsgroup will have a similar address revealing its type and topic. The following categories will aid in determining which of the nearly ten thousand newsgroups are worth investigating:

Category	Meaning
Alt.	Alternative themes (Most groups relating to history carry the Alt. designation)
Comp.	Computer-related topics
Misc.	Miscellaneous themes
News.	Posts about news groups
Rec.	Recreational topics
Sci.	Scientific discussions
Soc.	Social concerns
Talk.	Talk radio–style format

Reading and Posting Messages on Discussion Lists

Discussion lists are a hybrid of e-mail and newsgroups. With discussion lists, the posts and replies that anyone can access in newsgroups are sent by e-mail only to those who have subscribed to the list. As with most newsgroups, there is an editor who screens the posts before they are sent to subscribers, maintaining quality and decency. There are discussion lists that target students, professors, editors, publishers, librarians, and general readers. Almost any historical topic imaginable has a list devoted to it. How open the discussion lists are to subscribers is determined by the moderators. Some limit membership to those with a special interest, while others permit anyone who wishes to join. Chapter 2 discusses the lists focusing on history and explains their qualifications for subscription in more detail.

Chapter 2 will also provide more specific instructions on how to subscribe to each group. All discussion lists share a basic subscription format, however. To subscribe (or to unsubscribe), one simply sends an e-mail message to the computer that receives and distributes the messages. This computer is called the listserver (or listserv) because it serves the list. For example, to send a message to a list discussing the history of dogs (H-Dog), one would send the e-mail message

Subscribe H-Dog yourfirstname yourlastname
to the e-mail address: Listserv@ucbeh.san.uc.edu

The listserv would quickly acknowledge your registration as a member, and e-mail posts from the other list members would begin arriving in your box.

You should be careful only to join subscription lists that are truly of interest, and be certain to read your e-mail several times a week. Most discussion lists are very active, sending out fifteen or more messages per day. If you get carried away at first, you may find yourself buried under an avalanche of several hundred e-mail posts awaiting your eager attention. So be careful to only subscribe to those lists that most interest you until you gain a feel for how much mail you are likely to receive.

Logging Onto a Remote Computer with Telnet

Anyone who has ever used an electronic library catalog is familiar with the computerless screens and keyboards that allow patrons to access the library's catalog. These machines do not have their own microprocessors, but are linked to a central computer which shares information with all of the terminals connected to it. Telnet is a program offered by all Internet service providers that permits your home or office computer to act just like the terminals at the library. It enables you to temporarily connect to a remote computer and access its information as if it were on your own computer. Those interested in history will find Telnet particularly important because almost every major library in the world now allows Telnet access to its catalogs. Anyone can do subject searches or find out which libraries possess a specific work they are looking for.

Transferring Files with File Transfer Protocol (FTP)

File Transfer Protocol (or FTP) is similar to Telnet. Like Telnet, it is a program that connects you to a remote computer. FTP does not allow you to read the material on the remote machine; rather, it actually allows you to copy the files or programs and transfer them to your own computer. You can use FTP to get a copy of the United States Constitution or to download (as retrieving information with FTP is called) a program that teaches you the history of the Vietnam War. Thousands of sites with downloadable files, programs, and historical information are out there waiting to be tapped. Many of the best and most useful FTP sites will be discussed in Chapter 2.

As with Telnet, there are many packages that permit FTP access. For now, we will only mention that there are three main types of FTP access: anonymous FTP, identified FTP, and restricted FTP. Anonymous FTP allows anyone to connect to a computer and download information without giving an identity. Identified FTP also allows anyone to copy materials, but it requires you to give your e-mail address and name so that the sponsors of the site can maintain statistical information about the use of their site. Restricted FTP is used by some commercial and private institutions that only allow FTP for a fee or to authorized users. The sites mentioned in chapter 2 specify which of these categories the sites fall into and explain how to gain access when a fee or password is required.

Browsing the World Wide Web

For most computer users, time on the Internet will mean exploring the World Wide Web (WWW) and working with a Web browser (as the programs that allow access to the WWW are called). The Web is the most popular and fastest growing section of the Internet because it combines text, sound, and graphics to create multimedia sites. History buffs can find everything from an audio track of the *Battle Hymn of the Republic* to short film clips of JFK's assassination to a complete version of the French *Encyclopédie*. The most powerful Web browsers also perform all of the other Internet functions such as e-mail, Telnet, and FTP, so new users need only master one basic software package.

The Web and Web browser packages owe much of their popularity and potential to their multimedia format, but they also profit from their ability to link information. Web page developers can create links to any other page on the Web so that by merely using your mouse to point at a highlighted image or section of text and then clicking the correct mouse button, your computer can almost instantly bring up that information. Thus, a link on a home page (the first page of information you see when you connect to a Web site is called the home page) can connect you to any other site, just as a cross reference in a textbook sends you to other related information. This makes the WWW an amazingly easy-to-use source of information or recreation (for those who become Web junkies).

The next section discusses the software that makes connecting to the Web possible, but as with e-mail, you will need to understand Web addresses to find information on the WWW. These addresses are called URLs—uniform resource locators—which is simply techno-talk for addresses. Every page on the Web has a unique URL. This makes it very easy to go directly to the information you need. They look something like this:

http://www.uc.edu/www/history/reviews.htmlx.

Some addresses are longer than this. Some are shorter. All contain three basic parts. Looking from right to left, the first designation you notice is reviews.html. This tells you that you are retrieving a file called reviews in the html format. HTML (Hypertext Markup Language) is the standard language of the Web for saving multimedia information. Other possibilities include .gif and .jpeg, which indicate graphic images files, .avi and .wav, which indicate audio files, or .mov, which signals a movie.

The middle part of the address—/www.uc.edu/www/history/—is just like an e-mail address, specifying which network and computer stores the information so that your software package can find it on the Internet. The .edu extension tells you the information is at an educational institution, and as with e-mail, there will always be a three-letter code revealing the type of institution that sponsors the site.

The http:// lets you know that the browser is using the Hypertext Transfer Protocol to get the information. This is the standard language that governs the transfer and sharing of information on the Web. If you were using your browser to Telnet or FTP, the http:// would be replaced by ftp:// or telnet:// and then the address, showing which function your computer is performing.

Of course, you can use the Internet and profit from the World Wide Web without spending hours studying their technical background, history, and terms. The next section tells you how to get on the Internet and what software you need.

Getting On the Internet

Once upon a time, getting connected to the Internet was the hardest part of going on-line. In the early days, if you did not work for the military or a research institution, you were out of luck. The introduction of commercial providers in the 1980s made access easier to obtain, but it might cost you as much as a new car. Today, there are thousands of local and national Internet service providers, and the competition has made Internet access amazingly inexpensive. In most markets, you can now get almost unlimited access for $10 or $15 per month. For those fortunate enough to work for a library, college, university, or publisher, the price is often even better—free. Getting on the Internet has never been easier or less expensive.

Internet access is offered by three basic categories of service providers—corporate/institutional, national commercial, and local commercial providers. For those who work at companies or institutions offering Internet access to their employees, the best way to learn about your options is to speak directly to your system manager or computer support staff.

For those who do not have access to the Internet at work or school, there are several factors to consider in choosing a provider. Perhaps most important is finding a service that offers a local phone number or a toll-free number, so that you need not pay long-distance charges for your Internet access. The attractiveness of the Internet vanishes quickly in the presence of a $400 phone bill. Fortunately, there are now so many service providers it is usually easy to find a provider that offers a local phone number in your area.

The second consideration is the type of service you desire. Many local service providers in your city or state will offer almost unlimited access to the WWW, e-mail, FTP, and other basic services for very affordable rates ($5 to $20 a month). (Local service providers can be found by looking in your local phone book under "Internet Service

Providers" or "World Wide Web Service Providers.") There are also several national service providers such as America Online, CompuServe, and Prodigy, which provide special services in addition to basic Internet access. These services include such things as access to electronic versions of national newspapers, up-to-the-minute stock market reports, and special discussion lists and newsgroups available only to subscribers. Because these national service providers offer features you cannot find elsewhere, they are more expensive. The best way to decide if any of the national service providers feature packages you want is to contact each of them directly, keeping a record of the benefits and limitations of each service. A brief sketch of the three most popular national services is given below.

America Online (AOL)

According to industry statistics, America Online is the fastest growing national service provider, with more than two million users. AOL features members-only reference sections dedicated to games, news, sports, weather, and technical support, and it sponsors hundreds of members-only newsgroups and discussion lists. AOL also features many popular chat sessions in which members interested in a common theme can use their computer to "chat" (as if on the telephone) with celebrities, government figures, or other personalities.

AOL provides its own software for accessing the Internet. The software is attractive, easy to use, and includes all of the major Internet tools and services such as FTP, the Web, and Telnet. AOL also offers strong support for users with 28.8 kbs modems, and it has local phone numbers in most United States cities.

Free trial hours: 10–15
Monthly fee: $9.95
Monthly Internet hours without charge: 5
Additional hourly rate: $2.95
For more information, contact America Online at:
8619 Westwood Center Drive
Vienna, VA 22182–2285

1–800–827–6364
E-Mail: info@aol.com

CompuServe

CompuServe is the oldest and most developed of the major national service providers. It offers all of the same basic and special features as AOL, plus it has a very strong international presence. With local dialup numbers in cities around the globe, CompuServe provides the best service for those who travel internationally. CompuServe's Internet software package is also very easy to use and understand. It comes with detailed instructions and a tutorial that walks new users through its operation. Like AOL, CompuServe provides access to users with 28.8 kbs modems or any slower speed.

Free trial hours: First month
Monthly fee: $9.95
Monthly Internet hours without charge: Unlimited for basic services; 3 hours for Internet services
Additional hourly rate: $2.50
For more information, contact CompuServe at:
5000 Arlington Center Boulevard
P.O. Box 20212
Columbus, OH 43220
1–800–848–8990
E-Mail: postmaster@csi.compuserve.com

Prodigy

Prodigy provides the same types of service as AOL and CompuServe. It does not have CompuServe's international presence, but for access within the United States, it is a first-rate provider. One slight drawback to Prodigy is the high number of advertisements that clutter many pages of its basic and Internet menus. Prodigy's software is as easy to use as that of AOL and CompuServe, however. Prodigy also provides support for all speeds of modems.

Free trial hours: First month

Monthly fee: $9.95 regular plan; $14.95 value plan; $30 plan for 30 hours

Monthly Internet hours without charge: 5 in regular plan

Additional hourly rate: $2.95

For information, contact Prodigy at 1–800–776–3449

Hardware

Convenient use of the Internet and its many tools is governed by speed. The faster your computer can send and process information, the more pleasurable and productive your time on the Net will be. Thus, there is a simple rule of thumb that guides the purchase of computer equipment for use on the Internet: Buy the best machine you can realistically afford. This does not mean to mortgage your house just to get better equipment. Machines with the minimum configurations listed in Tables 1.1 and 1.2 will allow you to easily access the resources of the Internet. More memory (RAM), a faster processor, and a speedier modem will all enable you to interact with the Net more quickly, however. If you want to start with the basic system described below and gradually upgrade, make sure the first addition you make is more RAM. Upgrading from 4 megs to 8 or 16 megs of RAM or more will make the most noticeable difference in the performance of your computer. Improving your processor should be second and trading in your old modem should be done last. At present, the speed of phone lines restricts the effectiveness of modems, so you will get the least improvement in your system from the purchase of a faster modem.

Table 1.1

IBM Configurations

Processor	386/25 mhz or faster
RAM	4 MB or more
Modem	14.4 kbs or faster
Hard Drive	Required
Mouse	Required
VGA Monitor	Required

Software

While many educational institutions and the national service providers such as AOL, CompuServe, and Prodigy offer their own software packages with directions and tutorials, those who choose local service providers can select the software they wish to use to access the Internet. Most local service providers will also give new users software needed to access the Internet along with detailed instructions. In principle, however, you can use any package you wish to connect to the Internet through a local provider. This section will present brief descriptions of some of the best packages and explain where to obtain them.

Netscape and Mosaic

The two powerhouse packages (Web browsers, as they are called) that most Internauts use are Netscape and Mosaic. They combine all the tools for accessing the Web, sending e-mail, Telnetting, and using FTP. Both can display the combinations of graphics and text that make the Internet a lively and exciting resource, and both are simple to use and come with tutorials and a help feature. Developed by the National Center for Supercomputing Applications (NCSA) at the University of Illinois, Mosaic was the first graphical Web browser, and it contributed substantially to the popularization of the Internet. Netscape has recently become the industry leader, however, setting the standard for new features as the Internet evolves. Both software packages are good choices for all users from novices to experts.

Table 1.2

Apple Configurations

Processor	86030/25 mhz or faster
RAM	6 MB or more
Modem	14.4 kbs or faster
Hard Drive	Required
Mouse	Required
VGA Monitor	Required

Netscape and Mosaic are both available on the Internet. You can download Netscape by FTP at any of the following addresses (please note, addresses are case sensitive):

> ftp.netscape.com/netscape1.1/ (This is Netscape Corporation's FTP site, and it is usually extremely busy. You may wish to try one of the other sites.)
> ftp.cps.cmich.edu/pub/netscape
> ftp.utdallas.edu/pub/netscape/netscape1.1/
> magic.umeche.maine.edu/pub/Mirrors/nscape/

Mosaic can be downloaded by FTP at

> ftp.ncsa.uiuc.edu/Mosaic/

Both Netscape and Mosaic are currently available free for students, faculty, and staff of educational institutions and to employees of non-profit organizations. Others are asked to pay a small registration fee after a complimentary evaluation period. This fee is currently $39.

Eudora and Pegasus

Both Netscape and Mosaic perform all of the functions you need to explore the Internet, including e-mail. However, those who send and receive a lot of electronic correspondence, or who plan to send long files along with their messages, may prefer to use a package designed specifically to handle electronic mail. Eudora and Pegasus are currently the two best packages for handling e-mail that are available on the Internet. Both packages can send messages to lists of recipients, can send files in addition to or along with text, and feature attractive graphic environments and menus that make them easy to use.

Eudora is available via FTP at

> ftp.qualcomm.com/quest/eudora/windows/1.4

Pegasus is available via FTP at

> ftp.pegasus.com/pegasus

Both packages are available for free use to students, faculty, and staff of educational institutions. Others are asked to send a registration fee after a trial period.

Netiquette and Copyright

Because electronic communication is still new, the rules governing on-line expression are still evolving. There are already, however, some basic courtesies that help keep the free and open communication of the Internet polite and enjoyable. With this in mind, here are some Netiquette hints that can help keep you from accidentally offending someone.

General Netiquette

The most important thing to remember is that Internet communication is just like writing a letter. Electronic messages can be seen by many individuals other than the intended recipient. They can be forwarded to countless people. They can even be printed and posted in public areas. Thus, the golden rule of Internet communication should never be forgotten:

Never write anything you would not want a stranger to read.

It is also important to remember that e-mail is judged by the same standards as other written communication. Sometimes, the ease and speed of electronic communication lulls users into forgetting to check grammar and spelling. This can lead to your e-mail's being forwarded to thousands of individuals, and you do not want people all over the Internet laughing because you innocently asked if it was Vasco da Gama who circumcised the world with a 40-foot clipper.

There are also several special grammatical conventions that govern the Internet. One important rule is NOT TO WRITE EVERYTHING OUT IN CAPITAL LETTERS or to underline everything, *italicize everything,* or **to put everything in bold.** Seasoned e-mail readers consider this the equivalent of shouting at the top of your lungs, and it is considered the mark of a "newbie," or someone who has not yet learned to behave themself on the Internet.

Because e-mail lacks a convenient way to convey emotion through text, you will often encounter special symbols in e-mail correspondence. For example, a :) or :(is often put after a sentence to express happiness or sadness. A :0 may be added to express surprise. A :; may be inserted to indicate confusion, and history buffs who think they are Abe Lincoln may include a =|:-)= somewhere in their messages. These symbols add a bit of charm to Internet communication, but it is important to remember that they are only appropriate in informal correspondence. They also should not be overdone. Too many emotive symbols are considered to be another mark of a newbie.

Rules for Newsgroup and Discussion List Posts

Besides the Netiquette governing general Internet communication, there are also some rules for those who wish to participate in newsgroups and discussion lists.

1. Before you make a post to a group or list, it is wise to follow the group's posts for a while. This will help you to know what has already been asked and what type of questions/statements are considered appropriate. Asking repetitive or uninformed questions can get you off to a bad start.

2. Think before you write. Do not send off emotional or ill-considered responses to posts. (This is called "flaming" in Internet parlance.) Take time to consider criticisms, sarcasms, and insults carefully. Remember the Internet is not an anonymous frontier, and on-line remarks can be just as hurtful to a person as any others.

3. Do not send private correspondence to groups or lists. If you just want to thank someone, send the message to the person directly. And be very careful when you reply to a message. You do not want to accidentally tell several thousand readers about your date last night because you replied to the wrong address.

4. Do not post advertisements to groups or lists. This is considered extremely rude and intrusive, and it is the surest way to become the victim of vicious flaming. Internauts are being careful to avoid the spread of junk mail to the Internet.

Copyright

The question of copyright is an important one for students, teachers, librarians, publishers, and all those on the Internet. Everyone wants to know the laws governing copying and sharing information on the Internet, and lawyers and lawmakers are working to develop clear rules that govern electronic mediums. For now, the issues of copyright as they pertain to the Internet are still somewhat hazy, but there are some certainties that can guide your steps.

Most importantly, all on-line correspondence, files, and documents are handled like other written documents. They are automatically held to be copyrighted in the individual author's name. When an Internet item is copyrighted by some other party, the copyright holder generally is identified at the end of the document.

Students, teachers, and general users will be glad to know that a judge has just ruled that Internet documents can be copied according to the fair use rules that govern printed sources. You can make personal copies of on-line documents and images, and you can incorporate them in instructional packages (if you are a student, teacher, or librarian) as long as the package is in no way intended to generate a profit. Other more precise rules governing copyright will undoubtedly be developed in the near future. For now, the safest course seems to be treating Internet sources just like other written documents.

Chapter Two

Internet Sites for Historians

The history sites on the Internet present an astounding amount of information. No one could ever hope to view and read everything that is now on-line. Of course, no one could ever read every book in the Library of Congress either. This is why the Library of Congress is meticulously organized and cataloged. When you need to find a book or fact, you can go to an index or turn to a librarian for assistance. Since there is no Internet librarian, this section of *The History Highway* is designed to help you find specific information when you are looking for it and guide you to interesting and useful sites that are worth examining just for pleasure.

As you read this guide, you will notice that the historical sites on the Internet have been created by a wide variety of people, ranging from history professors and students to publishers and history buffs. There is also a broad range of content on the Internet. Some sites are scholarly; others are more informal. Some are composed entirely of links to other sites. Each entry in chapter 2 will provide an indication of the site's content. You will also find that sites generally are sponsored by four different sources that can offer clues to their nature:

1. *Collective Projects.* At some universities there are ongoing projects to collect and provide definitive electronic collections of materials on a certain topic. For example, the Perseus Project from Tufts

University has collected thousands of photographs of ancient Greek architecture, art, and pottery. Such a tremendous project would not be possible without the financial backing of a university or research grant and the help of a small army of graduate assistants.

2. *Government Information.* The government is using the Internet to publish materials that have been stashed away in archives where the public has had only limited access to them. Through the Internet they can now provide electronic access to these materials, which include letters, diaries, government documents, photographs, and film clips.

3. *Individual Projects.* Historians, archaeologists, theologians, and other scholars have used the Internet to post formal results of their research. Others have begun to use the Internet as a place to display items from their private collections, such as old family diaries, collections of eighteenth-century newspapers, or archives of folk songs. These sorts of sites can provide access to primary source material that might otherwise never have seen the light of day.

4. *Educators.* Many professors and teachers are incorporating the Internet into their course plans. They post their lesson plans, syllabi, and class assignments. Others go further and are making use of the Internet's unique technological features to encourage their students to post on-line commentaries or engage in interactive exercises on the Net. Some classes are being taught entirely over the Internet and are available to anyone who wishes to sign up. Often these classes are free, although some involve a fee.

As you navigate the Net, you will notice that new sites are being created daily, familiar sites disappear, and addresses occasionally change. Every effort has been made to provide the most up-to-date information available at the time of publication. The Internet is a rapidly growing and evolving place, however. Readers of *The History Highway* need not fear losing touch with their favorite sites or worry about missing the best new pages. *The History Highway* has its own World Wide Web site at http://www.uc.edu/www/history/highway.html, which will indicate the sites that have changed their addresses since publication and that will describe valuable new sites as they come along. Please help us to improve *The History Highway* and keep it up-to-date by sending suggestions and notices of new or changed sites to Trinklds@ucunix.san.uc.edu

GENERAL HISTORY

A Walk Through Time

http://physics.nist.gov/GenInt/Time/time.html

A Walk Through Time is an interesting look at the history of time-keeping. Beginning with an explanation of various ancient calendar systems, the site then discusses early clocks such as sundials and waterclocks, modern timekeeping methods, and time zones.

Archnet

http://spirit.lib.uconn.edu/ArchNet/ArchNet.html

gopher://spirit.lib.uconn.edu 70

At the main Gopher menu, choose: Academiç Subjects and Services

Archnet contains archaeological field reports, images, conference information, electronic exhibits, fieldwork opportunities, and more. It covers archaeology throughout the world, and the site is an excellent way to learn about field practices and the scholarship of historical archaeology.

Arctic Circle

http://www.lib.uconn.edu/ArcticCircle/index.html

Arctic Circle presents information on the history and culture of the Arctic regions. The site focuses on the people of the Arctic, but there is also much information on the natural resources and environment of the area.

ArtServ: Art and Architecture

http://rubens.anu.edu.au/

ArtServ provides access to sixteen thousand images relating to the history of art and architecture around the world.

Bill Douglas Centre for the History of Cinema and Popular Culture

http://www.ex.ac.uk/bill.douglas/

This archive houses the Bill Douglas and Peter Jewell Collection which is located at the University of Exeter and contains over sixty thousand items, including twenty-five thousand books and thousands of films.

Book Arts and Book History on the World Wide Web

http://www.cua.edu/www/mullen/bookarts.html

Book Arts and Book History on the World Wide Web is a gateway to Internet sites dealing with book history.

Britannica's Lives

http://www.eb.com/cgi-bin/bio.pl

Britannica's Lives gives brief biographical sketches of famous and infamous people born on the current day.

Databases

http://cs.muohio.edu/

Affiliated with H-Net, this is the Web site of the Databases discussion list. Their site discusses the design and management of historical databases. It also contains information about the discussion list and allows one to subscribe. There are conference announcements, bibliographies, reviews, articles, and links to related sites.

E Pluribus Unum: Out of Many, One

http://www.rtis.com/nat/user/coins/

E Pluribus Unum is an excellent home page on the study and collection of old coins. It includes essays on mintages, trading tips, collection suggestions, and access to a software program designed for constructing a coin database.

Eighteenth-Century Resources

http://www.english.upenn.edu/~jlynch/18th/

Eighteenth-Century Resources contains a wide variety of material on the eighteenth century from electronic texts to calls for papers. There is a large collection of digitized primary sources and many links to other sites.

Eighteenth-Century Studies

http://english-www.hss.cmu.edu/18th.html

This interdisciplinary site focuses on eighteenth-century literary and cultural studies. There are also many links to historical sources, and the site allows visitors to communicate with others who are interested in the period.

En Garde!

http://www.gt.kth.se/~bjornh/eg/

En Garde! is a clever interactive on-line game that combines history, an Errol Flynn movie, and a lot of role playing. It sets you in the seventeenth century and challenges you to climb the social ladder, teaching European history as you play.

Famous Libertarian and Anarchist Biographies

http://tigerden.com/~berios/libertarians.html

Famous Libertarian and Anarchist Biographies has extensive biographical information about prominent nineteenth- and twentieth-century anarchists, socialists, pacifists, and libertarians. There are also many links to related sites.

Galaxynet

http://galaxy.einet.net/galaxy/Social-Sciences/History.html

Galaxynet is a large, searchable database of links to sites on all subjects. This address takes you to Galaxynet's links to history sites.

The Gargantuan Virtual Guide to Cyber History

http://www.quiknet.com/~merlin

The Gargantuan Virtual Guide to Cyber History is the creation of Joel Walsh, a student in computer science at California State University–Sacramento. Walsh's site has nothing to do with Rabelais, but it contains links to many resources on the history of computers. There is also a lot of information about computer history that Walsh has gathered himself.

Gateway to World History

http://neal.ctstateu.edu/history/world_history/index.html

As its name implies, this site is a collection of links to pages on all aspects of world history. The links are indexed by topic, country, and subregion.

The Geological Time Machine

http://physics.nist.gov/GenInt/Time/time.html

Fans of Jurassic Park will love this site. The Geological Time Machine is a tour through the scholarship of historical geology and paleontology.

Global.change

http://cs.muohio.edu/

This is the Web site of the Global.change discussion list. Affiliated with H-Net, this group focuses on the historical role of economic forces in global change. Their Web pages contain information about the discussion list and allow one to subscribe. They also include calls for papers, conference announcements, bibliographies, book reviews, articles, and links to related sites.

Great Books of Western Civilization

http://www.ilinks.net/~lnoles/grtbks.html

This site is arranged around eight "great books" courses that Mercer University offers. Each section has a course description and full electronic versions of the texts used for the course.

Guide to Maritime History Information on the Internet

http://ils.unc.edu/maritime/home.html

The Guide to Maritime History Web page provides general information on all aspects of maritime history, including ships, music, art, and nautical archaeology.

Guide to Non-Western History

http://execpc.com/~dboals/hist.html

The Guide to Non-Western History site is primarily a collection of links. It sends you to a wide variety of general history sites, electronic journals, and K–12 resources.

Gypsy Lore Society

http://hamp.hampshire.edu/~ratS88/gls

The Gypsy Lore Society home page connects readers to information about the society and to related Web sites.

H-Anzau

http://h-net2.msu.edu/~anzau

This is the Web site of the H-Anzau discussion list, which is sponsored by the Economic History Society of Australia and New Zealand. The society's Web pages contain information about its discussion list, and the site allows one to subscribe. It also includes calls for papers, conference announcements, bibliographies, book reviews, articles, and links to related sites.

H-Business

http://h-net2.msu.edu/~business

Sponsored by H-Net, this site is the Web page of the H-Business discussion list. The Web site includes information about the discussion list and allows for subscription. It also has links to a wide array of business and commerce history resources.

H-Demog

http://h-net2.msu.edu/~demog

Sponsored by H-Net, this site is the Web page of the H-Demog discussion list. The Web site includes information about the discussion list and allows for subscription. It also has links to a wide array of demographic history resources.

H-Diplo

http://h-net2.msu.edu/~diplo

This site is the H-Net–supported Web page of the H-Diplo discussion list, which is dedicated to diplomatic history. The Web site includes information about the discussion list and allows for subscription. It also has links to a wide array of diplomatic history resources.

H-Film

http://h-net2.msu.edu/~film

This site is the Web page of the H-Net–sponsored H-Film discussion list, which is dedicated to cinema history. Its site contains information about the discussion list and allows one to subscribe. It also includes calls for papers, conference announcements, bibliographies, book reviews, articles, and links to related sites.

H-Grad

http://h-net2.msu.edu/~grad

This site is the Web page of the H-Net–sponsored H-Grad discussion list. H-Grad focuses on all the issues that concern graduate students in history. The site contains information about the discussion list and allows one to subscribe. It also includes job listings, fellowship and grant opportunities, calls for papers, conference announcements, articles, and links to related sites.

H-Ideas

http://h-net2.msu.edu/~ideas

Sponsored by H-Net, this is the Web site of the H-Ideas discussion list, which treats intellectual history. The site contains information about the discussion list and allows one to subscribe. It also includes calls for papers, conference announcements, bibliographies, book reviews, articles, and links to related sites.

H-Net Home Page

http://h-net2.msu.edu/

H-Net is a National Endowment for the Humanities–sponsored project to bring the humanities into the twenty-first century. H-Net's home page contains links to the more than seventy discussion lists they sponsor, to the Web pages of each of those discussion lists, to their extensive book review project, and to hundreds of other resources for historians.

H-Rhetor

http://h-net2.msu.edu/~rhetor

Sponsored by H-Net, this is the Web site of the H-Rhetor discussion list, which is dedicated to the history of rhetoric and communications. The site contains information about the discussion list and allows one to subscribe. It also includes calls for papers, conference announcements, bibliographies, book reviews, articles, and links to related sites.

H-State

http://h-net2.msu.edu/~state

This is the Web site of the H-State discussion list. This H-Net–sponsored group does not study local or state history as one might presume. Rather, it focuses on the history of the welfare state. Its Web pages contain information about the discussion list, and the site allows one to subscribe. It also includes calls for papers, conference announcements, bibliographies, book reviews, articles, and links to related sites.

H-Women

http://h-net2.msu.edu/~women

This is the Web site of the H-Women discussion list. Affiliated with H-Net, this group focuses on women's history. Its Web pages contain information about the discussion list, and the site allows one to subscribe. It also includes calls for papers, conference announcements, course suggestions, syllabi, bibliographies, book reviews, articles, and links to related sites.

H-World

http://h-net2.msu.edu/~world

This is the Web site of the H-World discussion list. Affiliated with H-Net, this group focuses on world history. Its Web pages contain information about the discussion list, and the site allows one to subscribe. It also includes calls for papers, conference announcements, bibliographies, book reviews, articles, and links to related sites.

Historical and Literary Graphics

http://web.syr.edu/~fjzwick/gbrowse/gbrowse.html

Historical and Literary Graphics is a large database of on-line images relating to all fields of history.

Historical Costuming

http://www.vmedia.com/books/ira/data/sect35/list1.htm

Historical Costuming is an attractively constructed Web site. It offers downloadable historical patterns, guides to historical authentication, tips on finding supplies, and information on early textiles and their modern equivalents.

History

http://www.execpc.com/~dboals/hist-gen.html

This site offers an annotated listing of general history links.

History Computerization Project

http://www.directnet.com/history

Sponsored by the University of Southern California and the Los Angeles City Historical Society, the History Computerization Project is a history information network for the exchange of information between historians, libraries, archives, museums, preservation groups, and historical societies. The project has created a database drawn from the collections of thousands of historical organizations, repositories, and universities. The material available includes photographs, museum objects, archives, books, journals, and oral history interviews.

History Departments Around the World

http://web.gmu.edu/departments/history/research/depts.html

This is an alphabetical listing of links to history department home pages in the United States and foreign countries. It is managed and updated by the students and faculty of the George Mason University history department.

History of Film, Video, and Television

http://www.soundsite.com/history/filmhis.html

This site offers a collection of general histories and information on film, video, and television. It also has excellent links to related materials.

History of Money from Ancient Times to the Present Day

http://www.ex.ac.uk/~RDavies/arian/llyfr.html

This is an interesting collection of essays on a range of topics dealing with money and currency. The topics include "Warfare and Financial History," "The Significance of Celtic Coinage," "The Third World and Debt in the Twentieth Century" and "The Origins of Money and Banking."

History of Philosophy

http://www.jhu.edu/~phil/subfold/histphil.html#theTop

This site is a large database of Internet resources for historical philosophy that can be searched by philosopher's name or historical period.

The Horus History Links

http://www.ucr.edu/h-gig/

Created and maintained by history faculty members at the University of California, Riverside, Horus History Links is one of the best general gateways to historical Web sites. The Horus project contains links to more than one thousand sites, and it features excellent interactive graphics and a multimedia format.

HyperHistory On-line Project

http://www.hyperhistory.com/

The HyperHistory Project attempts to present world history as a flowing, illustrated timeline. In ten-year increments, major figures and events are presented with clickable biographies and descriptions. The project is still under construction.

Jewish Culture and History

http://www.igc.apc.org/ddickerson/judaica.html

This is a large collection of links to Jewish Culture and History pages. Among the sites presented are the H-Judaic home page, the on-line Gedenbuch, a list of on-line databases, a home page on Martin Buber, the Jewishnet, a tour of Israel, and the Israel Information Service. A short description of each site is included.

Joan's Witch Directory

http://www.ucmb.ulb.ac.be/~joan/witches/index.html

Joan's Witch Directory contains information on witchcraft trials from around the world, some historical diaries, letters, and testimonials, and links to other sites of interest.

Left-Wing Lingo, Ideologies, and History

http://www.dsausa.org/dsa/Docs/Lingo.html

Left-Wing Lingo traces the history of the Left from its roots in postrevolutionary France through modern eco-feminism. Created by J. Hughes, the site contains e-texts, provocative historical analyses, images, sound files, and much more.

The Literary HyperCalendar

http://www.yasuda-u.ac.jp/LitCalendar.html

The Literary HyperCalendar lists a series of significant happenings in literary history for each calendar day. In some cases it also provides links to related information.

Pirates of the Caribbean

http://tigger.cc.uic.edu/~toby-g/pirates.html

Pirates of the Carribbean aims to correct the misconceptions and myths surrounding pirates. The site contains historical articles, definitions of terms, numerous images, and links to related sites.

Research Institute for the Humanities

http://www.arts.cuhk.hk/His.html

This is an excellent gateway to general history sites developed by the University of Hong Kong's department of history. This site is a diverse and searchable guide to history links in all fields of history.

Shipwrecks and Shipwreck Recovery Articles

http://www.treasure.com/sasra.htm

This site contains full-text articles about shipwrecks from all periods, including articles about exploration, excavation, and preservation.

A Student Blooper History of Western Civilization

http://ark.resnet.cornell.edu/bloopers.html

This often reprinted history of western civilization is composed entirely of student bloopers gathered by teachers over the years. This site will not teach you much about history, but it's guaranteed to leave you laughing.

Tennessee Technological University History Resources

gopher://gopher.tntech.edu:70/11gopher_root%3A%5Bcampus.as.hist%5D

http://www.tntech.edu/www/acad/hist/history.html

Created by the Department of History at Tennessee Technological University, this is a good general starting point for gopher resources on the Internet, including essays on why one should study history and careers for historians.

University of Kansas History Resources

http://kuhttp.cc.ukans.edu/history/index.html

This site, sponsored by the University of Kansas, is one of the oldest and largest collections of links to sites on all topics of history. It is an excellent starting point for research.

"The White Man's Burden" and Its Critics

http://web.syr.edu/~fjzwick/kipling/whiteman.html

Rudyard Kipling's 1899 poem "The White Man's Burden" justified colonial imperialism, and it immediately generated a flood of responses. This site provides access to the full text of these poems, essays, cartoons, and interviews.

World Cultures to 1500

http://www.wsu.edu:8080/~dee/InternetResources.html

World Cultures to 1500 indexes links to subjects such as human language, the history of mathematics, and world art. It is a good source for Web pages on non-European history.

World History Archives

http://library.ccsu.ctstateu.edu/~history/world_history/archives/

The World History Archives are a repository for documents that encourage an understanding of world history and the struggle for social progress. There is a lot of information here relating to the Third World, global economic forces, women's liberation, socialism, and communism.

World History to 1500

http://www.byuh.edu/coursework/hist201/

This large gateway has excellent links to non-Western historical sites.

World Rulers

http://www.geocities.com/Athens/1058/rulers.html

World Rulers lists the past and present leaders of every state in the world. Birth and death dates are provided, as well as pictures for some. Monthly updates are posted.

ANCIENT HISTORY

Abzu

http://www.oi.uchicago.edu:80/OI/DEPT/RA/ABZU/ABZU.HTML

Abzu is a guide to the ancient Near Eastern resources that are available on the Internet. The materials include electronic journals, museum information, on-line exhibits, and links to other resources.

Acropolis

http://www.mechan.ntua.gr/webacropol/

This site features a virtual tour of the Acropolis.

Ancien-L

http://tanelorn.ncsa.uiuc.edu/ancien-l/ancien-l-archive.html

The Web page of the Ancien-L discussion list, this site allows one to join the list and contains an archive of all the posts that have been sent to Ancien-L.

Ancient City of Athens

http://www.indiana.edu/~kglowack/Athens/Athens.html

This is an impressive photographic tour of the city of Athens. The site is still under development and more pictures are being added, but the images already included are excellent. The pictures currently available show the Agora, parts of the Acropolis, the Pynx, and other ruins. Each picture is annotated with an informative description.

Ancient Egypt

http://www.memst.edu/egypt/egypt.html

This site takes visitors on a color tour of ancient Egypt. The graphics are first-rate, and each image is accompanied by an informative historical discussion.

Ancient Medicine/Medicina Antiqua

http://www.ea.pvt.k12.pa.us/medant/

Published by the Department of Classical Studies at the University of Michigan, this site contains a variety of resources concerning the study of Greco-Roman medicine and medical thought. It includes bibliographies, hypertexts, announcements, and a review section.

Ancient Roman Cooking

http://www.cs.cmu.edu/~mjw/recipes/ethnic/historical/ant-rom-coll. html

The Ancient Roman Cooking Web page presents a variety of ancient Roman recipes, including ways to prepare lamb, seafood, and fruit. It also features an encyclopedia of native Roman ingredients and a conversion chart to standard American and metric units of measure.

Ancient Texts

gopher://ccat.sas.upenn.edu:3333/11/Classical

Ancient Texts contains many classical works by classical authors, such as Aesop, Homer, and Sophocles.

The Ancient World Web

http://atlantic.evsc.virginia.edu/julia/AncientWorld.html

The Ancient World Web is an extensive guide to ancient history on the Internet created by University of Virginia librarian Julia Hayden. Like a good library resource, the database can be searched by location or subject. Some of the subjects covered include art, archaeology, law, and history. The subjects also go far beyond Rome and Greece; there is a wealth of information on ancient Australia, Guatemala, and Thailand, just to name a few of the places covered. This is an excellent starting point for ancient history research.

Anglo-Saxon Texts

ftp://ftp.std.com/WWW/obi/Anglo-Saxon

This is an FTP site for downloading or viewing historical Anglo-Saxon texts.

Archive of Watermarks and Papers in Greek Manuscripts

http://abacus.bates.edu/Faculty/wmarchive/

Produced by Robert Allison from Bates College and the Patriarchal Institute for Patristic Studies in Thessaloniki, this site contains an introduction, an overview, and a history of the archive. It also provides materials to allow for dating and establishing the provenance of Greek manuscripts.

The Aztec Calendar

http://napa.diva.nl/~voorburg/aztec.html

This site explains the two Aztec calendars: the 260-day sacred calendar and the 365-day secular calendar. There is a wealth of information about each calendar, and two software programs are available which allow you to display the calendars on your personal computer, convert from a Julian date to the corresponding Aztec date, and view the glyph symbols from several authentic Aztec calendars.

Barbarians on the Greek Periphery: Origins of Celtic Art

http://faraday.clas.virginia.edu/~umw8f/Cze/HomePage.html

Barbarians on the Greek Perhiphery examines the stylistic changes that took place in fifth-century Celtic art.

Classics and Mediterranean Archaeology

http://rome.classics.lsa.umich.edu/welcome.html

This site is primarily a gateway to sites dedicated to ancient history. The sites can be searched according to a variety of subjects, and there are some original articles.

Classics Alcove

http://nervm.nerdc.ufl.edu/~blaland/Class.html

Sponsored by the University of Florida, this site contains links to a great variety of resources, including journals, databases, images, instructional resources, and guides. Most are in English.

Diogenes' Links to the Ancient World

http://h16.snider.net/lyceum/

Visitors to Diogenes' Links will find mythological, anthropological, archaeological, literary, and art historical references to sites on ancient Mesopotamia, Egypt, Greece, Rome, and Assyria.

Diotima: Materials for the Study of Women and Gender in the Ancient World

http://www.uky.edu/ArtsSciences/Classics/gender.html

Diotima contains bibliographies, images, and articles for the study of women and gender in the ancient world.

Duke Papyrus Archives

http://odyssey.lib.duke.edu/papyrus/texts/homepage.html

This is an outstanding site providing access to texts and images of papyri from ancient Egypt. It includes information about conserving, interpreting, cataloging, and imaging papyri. There is a searchable catalog of over one thousand records from Duke University's Papyri Collection, full-text articles on the history of papyrology, and information about ancient writing systems.

Electronic Resources for Classicists:
The Second Generation
http://www.circe.unh.edu/Classics/resources.html

This is an annotated Web site edited by Maria C. Pantelia of the University of New Hampshire. It covers various aspects of the classics and ancient history.

Exploring Ancient World Cultures
http://eawc.evansville.edu/index.htm

This site is a gateway to ancient history Web sites on India, Egypt, China, Greece, the Near East, the Roman Empire, and the Islamic world. There are also many connections to sites on medieval Europe. Each culture is indexed separately, with each section preceded by a short introduction. Each list of sites is also well annotated.

Flint and Stone: Real Life in Prehistory
http://www.ncl.ac.uk/~nantiq/

This exhibition takes you into the lives of the inhabitants of Britain and northwestern Europe from the Ice Age to the advent of sedentary farming.

Greek and Roman Civilization Home Page
http://hermes.ucd.ie/~civilise/classics.html

The Greek and Roman Civilization Home Page contains links to resources covering the art, archaeology, and culture of Greece and Rome.

Guardian's Egypt Home Page
http://pages.prodigy.com/G/U/N/guardian/egypt.htm

The *Guardian*'s Egypt Home Page is an excellent collection of historical sketches, attractive images, and links to related sites.

Hellenic Civilization Database
http://www.greekcivil.ariadne-t.gr/default.html

The Hellenic Civilization Database is a large collection of links, including connections to Greek arts and literature and more than two hundred museums.

Hellenic Civilization Gopher

gopher://ithaki.servicenet.ariadne-t.gr/

This large database contains information on Greek civilization, literature, maritime museums, and theatrical museums. There is also information in audio and textual format.

Imperium Romanorum

http://wwwtc.nhmccd.cc.tx.us:443/people/crf01/rome/

Developed by Clifton Fox, a professor of history at Tomball College, this site contains lists of the officials of Rome arranged by year, a genealogical guide to the House of Caesar, and links to related material.

Library of the Age of Antiquity

http://www.uio.no/~aenersen/antiquity.html

The Library of the Age of Antiquity is a comprehensive index of ancient history, including links to sites for women, arts and crafts, literature, philosophy, and trivia.

Lupercalia

http://miso.wwa.com/~jase/lupercalia/history.html

This Web site contains a brief history and description of Lupercalia, the ancient Roman holiday celebrated on the ides of February. The site also contains links to other sites that treat Roman history.

Material Culture of the Ancient Canaanites, Israelites, and Related Peoples

http://staff.feldberg.brandeis.edu/~jacka/ANEP/ANEP.html

This site offers a searchable database of over one thousand images relating to the ancient Middle East. Most of the images are accompanied by historical and descriptive sketches.

Mayan Civilization Past and Present

http://indy4.fdl.cc.mn.us/~isk/maya.html

Mayan Civilization Past and Present links users to a wide range of historical, cultural, and archaeological sites that explore the Mayan civilization.

Mayan Epigraphic Database Project

http://jefferson.village.virginia.edu/med/home.html

The Mayan Epigraphic Database Project is compiling a collection of primary and secondary sources that show the evolution of Mayan script. The site includes a glyph catalog.

MayaQuest

http://mayaquest.mecc.com/MayaQuest.Home.html

gopher://informns.k12.mn.us:70/11/mn-k12/MAYAQUEST

MayaQuest is a good example of how the Internet can be used as a teaching tool. This project was launched in February of 1995 when a team of bicyclists traveled through Mexico's famous Mayan ruins. Thousands of classes logged in each week to track the cyclists, discuss the expedition with other participants and experts, and create and use curriculum resources. Although the expedition is over, the site and its rich materials are still available on-line.

Mesoamerican Archaeology World Wide Web Page

http://copan.bioz.unibas.ch/meso.html

The Mesoamerican Archaeology Page links users to on-line research, software, images, and reports relevant to Mesoamerican and pre-Columbian archaeology.

The Mystery of the Maya

http://www.cmcc.muse.digital.ca/membrs/civiliz/maya/mminteng.html

The Mystery of the Maya Web is a beautifully illustrated, on-line exhibition which explores Mayan history, culture, religion, and artifacts.

Paleolithic Cave Paintings in France

http://www.culture.fr/culture/gvpda-en.htm

This site discusses the paintings and engravings dating from the Paleolithic Age that have been found in the caves of Southern France. The material is in both French and English and includes excellent images of the cave paintings along with historical descriptions.

Papyrology Home Page

http://www-personal.umich.edu/~jmucci/papyrology/

The Papyrology Home Page houses images, scholarly resources, and links to institutions with an interest in papyrology.

The Perseus Project: Art and Archaeology

http://medusa.perseus.tufts.edu/

The Perseus Project Web site contains a massive library of art objects, sites, and buildings. Each entry has a description of the object and its context, as well as images. The catalog currently contains 523 coins, 1,420 vases, 366 sculptures, 179 sites, and 381 buildings. This is a searchable database, meaning that you can request, for example, "a listing of courthouses in Sicily dating from late antiquity." There are usually several photographs of each object from a variety of angles.

Project Runeberg

gopher://gopher.lysator.liu.se/

http://www.lysator.liu.se/runeberg

Project Runeberg is an initiative to collect and create electronic editions of classic Nordic literature and art.

Reeder's Egypt Page

http://www.sirius.com/~reeder/egypt.html

Created by Greg Reeder, this page examines the history of ancient Egypt. The site contains the Egyptian studies journal *KMT*, scholarly articles, and an on-line exhibit dedicated to the tombs of King Niusere's manicurists. There is also a good collection of links to related materials.

The Roman Empire

http://wwwtc.nhmccd.cc.tx.us:443/people/crf01/rome/

This site contains genealogical guides to the Caesars; a chronology of Roman emperors, consuls, and censors; and links to other relevant sites.

Romarch

http://www-personal.umich.edu/~pfoss/index.html

Created by Pedar Foss of the University of Michigan, Romarch contains a large array of historical resources on the Roman Empire. There is a clickable map of the empire which leads visitors to materials divided by location; one can link to museums, e-texts, image collections, historical articles, teaching resources, and other resources.

Rome Resources

http://www.nltl.columbia.edu/groups/Rome/index.html

The Rome Project is assembling a large database on classical Rome. At present, it includes articles on the literature, military, archaeology, politics, philosophy, drama, religion, and maps of the Roman Empire.

The Seven Wonders of the Ancient World

http://pharos.bu.edu/Egypt/Wonders/

Created by Alaa K. Ashmawy, this site presents a multimedia look at the Seven Wonders of the Ancient World. It contains discussions of art, history, trivia, and archaeological evidence. There are also many excellent links to related sites and additional images.

Tech Classics Archive

http://the-tech.mit.edu/Classics/index.html

The Tech Classics Archive contains nearly four hundred electronic texts which can be searched by author, title, date, or translator. It also offers links to related sites.

The Warfare and Tactics of the Roman Republic

http://www.ganet.net/~atulv/roman/index.html

This site describes the organization and procedures of the Roman army. It also discusses and analyzes Roman strategies in many important battles.

MEDIEVAL AND RENAISSANCE HISTORY

American Academy of Research Historians of Medieval Spain

http://kuhttp.cc.ukans.edu/kansas/aarhms/mainpage.html

The American Academy of Research Historians of Medieval Spain is an association of historians founded twenty years ago to exchange scholarly resources and ideas. This site includes links to discussion lists, translated documents, a reference area, and membership information for the academy.

Ancient and Medieval Coins

http://www_wwrc.uwyo.edu/coinnet/coinnet.html

This Web page presents information about the mint markings and metal content of ancient and medieval coins. The author of this page also provides you with the opportunity to send him a description of a coin, and he will try to identify it for you.

Anglo-Saxon England Before the Vikings

http://engserve.tamu.edu/files/linguistics/ling410/as/as.html

This is an essay on Anglo-Saxon history and culture, with supporting maps and pictures.

The Arte of Defense

http://mac9.ucc.nau.edu/fencing.html

The Arte of Defense is dedicated to fifteenth- and sixteenth-century fencing. It includes information on fencing masters from the period, terminology, equipment, and contemporary groups who take part in period fencing demonstrations.

Articles Concerned with the Middle Ages and the Renaissance

http://www-external.hal.com/~goldschm/articles.html

This site houses articles on unique and interesting aspects of the Middle Ages, such as writing systems, music, games, famous individuals, and religious history.

The Bayeaux Tapestry

http://blah.bsuvc.bsu.edu/bt

This site contains full-color images of the Bayeaux tapestry along with interpretative and explanatory text.

Book of Hours

http://acs1.byu.edu:80/~hurlbutj/dscriptorium/spalding/spalding.html

This Web site has twenty-five images from the Book of Hours, which was made for Marguerite de France on the occasion of her marriage in 1559.

A Brief History of Falconry

http://justice.loyola.edu/~rmcilhar/falconry/history.html

A history of falconry in various parts of the world.

The Camelot Project

http://rodent.lib.rochester.edu/camelot/cphome.htm

This is an excellent site developed at the University of Rochester. It presents scholarly Arthurian bibliographies; numerous articles on the figures, myths, and symbols of Arthurian lore; rich images; links to related sites; and a wealth of additional information.

CURIA: The Irish Manuscripts Project

http://curia.ucc.ie/curia/menu.html

The mission of the CURIA Project is to provide a searchable on-line database of literary and historical materials in the various languages of early, medieval, and modern Ireland.

Dante Project

http://www.ilt.columbia.edu/projects/dante/index.html

The Dante Project intends to provide multimedia versions of Dante's works that can serve as research and teaching tools. The site currently contains several original versions and translations of *The Divine Comedy* which are illustrated and accompanied by a hypertext-linked commentary.

The DILS Project

gopher://gopher.epas.utoronto.ca/11/cch/disciplines/medieval_studies /keefer

The DILS Project houses a database of manuscripts written in Anglo-Saxon England prior to 1100.

Florentine Renaissance Resources: On-Line Catasto of 1427

http://www.stg.brown.edu/projects/catasto/overview.html

This is an on-line version of the tax data for the city of Florence from 1427 to 1429. The site has its own search engine which helps users to find information for specific people, places, or topics.

Gargoyles Then and Now

http://ils.unc.edu/garg/garghp4.html

Gargoyles Then and Now is a wonderfully illustrated site that offers historical articles, a glossary, and a tour highlighting the gargoyles that can be found on cathedrals throughout Europe.

Gregorian Chant Home Page

http://www.music.princeton.edu:80/chant_html/

The Gregorian Chant page contains a wide variety of information on the history and practice of chant.

Hill Monastic Manuscript Library

http://www.csbsju.edu/hmml

The Hill Monastic Manuscript Library contains images from a variety of famous and little known manuscripts.

Hwaet! Old English in Context

http://www.georgetown.edu/cball/hwaet/hwaet06.html

Hwaet! presents lessons in basic Old English. It also includes links to sound files that will help one learn Old English.

La Renaissance

http://sunsite.icm.edu.pl/wm/paint/glo/renaissance/

La Renaissance discusses the philosophy, science, and social thought of the Renaissance in Italy, the Netherlands, Germany, and France.

Labyrinth: A WWW Server for Medieval Studies

http://www.georgetown.edu/labyrinth/

Labyrinth is the major scholarly clearinghouse for medieval resources on the Internet. Sponsored by Georgetown University, it has a searchable index which includes professional directories, on-line bibliographies, and subject-specific home pages. There are also links to special topics such as Arthurian studies and medieval music. The Labyrinth Library contains the full-text versions of medieval works in Latin, French, Italian, Old English, and Middle English.

Learning to Read Rome's Ruins

http://sunsite.unc.edu/expo/vatican.exhibit/exhibit/b-archeology/Arch aeology.html

Between 1450 and 1600, Renaissance scholars began to uncover the ruins of classical Rome. These scholars were fascinated by the emerging traces of their heritage, but they were not certain how to interpret the ruins they discovered. This site explores how archaeology was born as these Renaissance scholars struggled to study and understand their past.

Medieval and Renaissance Brewing Home Page

http://www.pbm.com/~lindahl/brewing.html

The Medieval and Renaissance Brewing Home Page contains authentic recipes for period drinks such as mead and raspberry cordials.

Medieval and Renaissance Clip Art

http://peg.pegasus.oz.au/~bblart/medieval.htm

The Medieval and Renaissance Clip Art page includes black and white as well as color clip art—graphic images that can easily be downloaded or cut and pasted into documents.

Medieval and Renaissance Embroidery

http://www.staff.uiuc.edu/~jscole/medembro.html

This Web site has information about the techniques of embroidery, as well as links to sites on famous tapestries.

Medieval and Renaissance Food Home Page

http://www.pbm.com/~lindahl/food.html

The Medieval and Renaissance Food Home Page provides many articles and recipes to help you re-create period dishes.

Medieval and Renaissance Wedding Information

http://paul.spu.edu/~kst/bib/bib.html

Everything you ever wanted to know about a medieval/Renaissance wedding but were afraid to ask. The topics covered include period ceremony, food, garb, invitations, and flowers. A bibliography of sources is also presented, and there are many links to related sites.

Medieval Books in Electronic Format

http://www.cs.cmu.edu/afs/andrew.cmu.edu/org/Medieval/www/src/medieval/periodbook.html

This site includes full-text versions of many medieval plays, letters, and poems which can be downloaded.

Medieval Spain

ftp://ftp.acns.nwu.edu/pub/NUacademics/hispanic.studies/index.html

This Web site contains full-text articles, bibliographies, and electronic texts relating to medieval Iberia.

Medieval Studies

gopher://gopher.epas.utoronto.ca/11/cch/disciplines/medieval_studies

Sponsored by the University of Toronto, this site contains bibliographies, e-texts, and articles. The site is especially rich on Chaucer.

The Middle English Collection at the University of Virginia

http://etext.virginia.edu/me.browse.html

This site contains full-text versions of many of the plays, poems, and philosophical writings contained in the Middle English Collection of the University of Virginia Library.

Old English Pages

http://www.georgetown.edu/cball/oe/old_english.html

Developed by Dr. Cathy Ball of Georgetown University, this site is an electronic primer on Old English. There are samples from Old English texts, translations of *Beowulf* and the Book of Genesis, manuscript images, on-line discussion groups, Old English fonts, instructional software, and links to Old English courses.

The Plague and Public Health in Renaissance Europe

http://jefferson.village.virginia.edu/osheim/intro.html

This site is a hypertext archive of scholarly articles, medical consilia, governmental records, religious writings, and images documenting the arrival, impact, and handling of various epidemic diseases in western Europe between 1348 and 1530.

Regia Anglorum: Anglo-Saxon, Viking, Norman, and British Living History

http://www.ftech.net/~regia/index.htm#index

Regia Anglorum is a large collection of articles on all aspects of medieval life, including brewing, embroidery, glasswork, pottery, housing, and furniture. There are also a number of articles on military concerns such as law, arms, armor, and Viking military organization.

Resources for the Medieval Historian

http://www.calpoly.edu/~jheinen/medieval.html

This Web page contains a large list of links dedicated to medieval history compiled by Dr. Jeff Heinen of California Polytechnic State University.

The Rune Typology Project

http://gonzo.hd.uib.no/NCCH-docs/runes.html

Sponsored by the Norwegian Research Council, this project's aim is to develop a transliteration system for Norwegian, Swedish, and Danish runes.

Secrets of the Norman Invasion

http://www.cablenet.net/pages/book/index.htm

The Secrets of the Norman Invasion contains more than sixty articles that debate the precise point where the Normans landed in England prior to the Battle of Hastings. The articles are divided into two categories. One group deals with the clues contained in primary source documents, while the other part looks at evidence from surveys, aerial photographs, walking tours, and archaeological work.

Sexual Relations in Renaissance Europe

http://www.tcd.net/~garn/sex.html

This site presents a broad look at sexuality during the Renaissance. The materials address issues ranging from sex and the Church to homosexuality and syphilis.

Statutes of Biella

http://kuhttp.cc.ukans.edu/ftp/pub/history/Europe/Medieval/latintexts/

This site provides access to legal codes from the Italian town of Biella which were written between 1248 and 1348. The codes offer an interesting glimpse into the social values of a medieval Italian town. They can be read in either Latin or English.

Treasures of the British Library

http://portico.bl.uk/access/treasures/overview.html

This is a collection of exhibits from the British Library highlighting its famous medieval and Renaissance collections. The exhibits rotate periodically. At the moment, the objects on display include the Diamond Sutra; the world's first printed document, which was produced in eighth-century China; the Magna Carta; the Lindisfarne Gospels; and some of Leonardo da Vinci's notebooks.

The Très Riches Heures du Duc de Berry

http://humanities.uchicago.edu/images/heures/heures.html

Considered by many to be the most beautiful medieval book of hours, the Très Riches Heures du Duc de Berry were crafted between 1412 and 1416. This site has commentary and color images of twelve of the illustrations.

Tutorial on Gregorian Chant

gopher://osiris.wu-wien.ac.at:7121/11/pub/earlym-l/gregorian.chants

This tutorial includes a series of essays that discuss the history, structure, syntax, and performance of Gregorian chant.

Tyburn Tree: Public Execution in Early Modern England

http://www.columbia.edu/~zll1/tyburn.html

The Tyburn Tree: Public Execution in Early Modern England site contains documents, images, bibliographies, and transcripts of last words.

The Viking Home Page

http://www.control.chalmers.se/vikings/viking.html

This Web page offers general information about the Viking era (defined here as 793–1066), including information about culture, recipes, ships, runestones, and the Viking journeys through Russia and America.

Vikings!

http://www.n-vision.com/spoon/vikes/index.html

This site has some unique information about Viking culture, including an entire section on Viking footwear, complete with drawings and information about craftsmanship. Other sections explain rank and status in the Viking world.

The World of the Vikings

http://www.demon.co.uk/history/index.html

The World of the Vikings includes information about runes, Viking sagas, and museums. There is also a large list of links to related sites.

WORLD HISTORY

AFRICA

Abyssinia CyberSpace Gateway

http://www.cs.indiana.edu/hyplan//dmulholl/acg.html

The Abyssinia CyperSpace Gateway celebrates the culture and people of northeast Africa. It includes photographs, general information, and mailing lists.

African Studies

http://www.w3.org/hypertext/DataSources/bySubject/AfricanStudies/africanWWW.html

This index is a major gateway for African studies links.

Center for African Studies at the University of Pennsylvania

http://www.sas.upenn.edu/African_Studies/AS.html

This University of Pennsylvania project has a wide variety of scholarly information concerning African studies.

Egyptian Government CultureNet Home Page

http://www.idsc.gov.eg/culture/index.htm

The Egyptian Government CultureNet Home Page contains articles and exhibits on all aspects of Egyptian history and culture. Egyptian museums and historic sites are discussed, and many links to other similar sites are listed.

Ethiopian Jewry

http://www.cais.com/nacoej/index.html

This Web page is dedicated to recounting the history, customs, and traditions of the Ethiopian Jews.

Great Zimbabwe

http://wn.apc.org/mediatech/VRZ10011.HTM

This site explores the mystery of Great Zimbabwe, the thirteenth-century fortress that has been the center of archaeological debate since its discovery.

University of Illinois Center for African Studies

http://wsi.cso.uiuc.edu/CAS/

The University of Illinois Center for African Studies home page, run by Professor Al Kagan, is a large gateway to sites of interest to historians of African studies.

Vanished Kingdoms of the Nile: The Rediscovery of Ancient Nubia

http://www.oi.uchicago.edu/OI/PROJ/NUB/NUBX92/NUBX92_brochure.html

Vanished Kingdoms of the Nile is a hypertext article about the history of ancient Nubia, complete with photographs, maps, and a bibliography.

ASIA AND THE MIDDLE EAST

Afghan History Links

http://frankenstein.worldweb.net/afghan/FaqNew/history.html

Afghan History Links presents a timeline history of Afghanistan from 2000 B.C. to 1996. The site is currently being revised.

Anatolia Through the Ages

http://yarra.vicnet.net.au/~focus/civi_mn1.htm

Anatolia Through the Ages gives a broad history of Anatolia. It covers the years 8000 B.C. through 1923.

Asian Studies on the Web

gopher://coombs.anu.edu.au:80/hGET%20/WWWVL-AsianStudies.
html

This Web page serves as a major clearinghouse for Asian resources, including the Middle East.

Cambodian Auto-Genocide Page

http://heart.engr.csulb.edu/cambodia/

The Cambodian Auto-Genocide Page discusses the atrocities committed by the Khmer Rouge and their impact upon the history of Cambodia. The site also offers many connections to related sites. Note that this page contains graphic text and images.

H-Asia

http://h-net2.msu.edu/~asia

Sponsored by H-Net, this site is the Web affiliate of the H-Asia discussion list. The site contains information about the discussion list and allows one to subscribe, but it also includes a great deal of information relating to Asian history. There are calls for papers, conference announcements, bibliographies, book reviews, articles, and links to related sites.

Jerusalem Mosaic

http://www1.huji.ac.il/jeru/jerusalem.html

Created by students at Hebrew University in Jerusalem, this site takes you on a historical tour of Jerusalem. The site is navigable by clickable maps and contains a wealth of assorted information in graphic, textual, and audio format. This site is truly a mosaic of Jerusalem's past and present.

Masks from Java

http://www.bvis.uic.edu/museum/exhibits/javamask/Icons1.html

Masks from Java includes photographs and texts describing the significance of several types of nineteenth-century masks from Java.

Philippine History

http://pubweb.acns.nwu.edu/~flip/history.html

This site provide a narrative account of the long history of the Philippine people.

A Philippine Leaf

http://www.bibingka.com/dahon

A Philippine Leaf is an interesting site about literacy and the written script in the ancient Philippines.

Turkish History

http://funnelweb.utcc.utk.edu/~utktsa/history.html

This site presents hypertext articles on the history of Turkey.

Zagarell's Archaeology Page

http://server.nextlab.cc.wmich.edu/~zagarell/

Zagarell's Archaeology Page discusses the current archaeological research being carried out in Iran and India.

China

The Art of War by Sun-Tzu

http://www.ChinaPage.com

The complete text of this sixth-century-B.C. classic is provided in the original Chinese, along with an English translation.

Center for Chinese Studies Library, Berkeley

http://www.lib.berkeley.edu/CCSL/

This page includes the center's catalog and bibliographic aids. It also lists hundreds of sites devoted to Chinese culture and history.

Chinese History and Culture

http://www.cernet.edu.cn/history.html

Chinese History and Culture presents a narrative history of China. There is also an electronic memorial for the victims of the rape of Nanking, a brief timeline of the Chinese dynasties, sound archives on the founding of the modern Communist state, and links to a host of related sites.

Hmong Culture and History Directory

http://www.stolaf.edu/people/cdr/hmong/

This Web page links visitors to a variety of sites on Hmong culture. Included are cultural events, news resources, mailing lists, publications on Hmong culture, photographic archives, and other links.

Missionaries and Mandarins: The Jesuits in China

http://www.task.gda.pl/expo/vatican.exhibit/exhibit/i-rome_to_china/ Jesuits_in_China.html

China was the focus of sixteenth- and seventeenth-century missionary activities for the Jesuits. In order to impress the Chinese with Western forms of knowledge, they translated into Chinese the classical works of cartography and astronomy in addition to Christian texts. This exhibit displays many of these manuscripts.

India

Indian Culture and History

http://www.webhead.com/wwwvl/India

This site focuses on modern Indian culture, but there is a variety of historical information as well as links to many history sites.

Japan

H-Japan

http://h-net2.msu.edu/~japan

Sponsored by H-Net, this is the Web site of the H-Japan discussion list. The site contains information about the discussion list and allows one to subscribe. It also includes calls for papers, conference announcements, bibliographies, book reviews, articles, and links to related sites.

History and Culture of Japan

http://www.pacificu.edu/up/as/japan.html

This site looks at all aspects of Japanese history and culture. It includes sections on cultural, economic, and landscape history along with many good links to related sources.

Japanese Surrender Documents, 1945

gopher://wiretap.spies.com/Gopher/Gov/US-History/japan.sur

This Web page is a collection of documents relating to the Japanese terms of surrender in 1945.

Pacific Century—History and Culture of Japan

http://www.uis.edu/~www/crowley/singapor.html

This site is an index of links on Japanese history, government, politics, and foreign relations.

EUROPE

General European History

Andorra

http://www.sigma.net/fafhrd/andorra/history.htm

Andorra provides a history of the world's smallest nation, a 450-square-kilometer territory located between France and Spain. The site also links users to information about the area, people, and economy of Andorra.

Austerlitz—The Battle of Three Emperors

http://www.bsf.cz/index/Austerlitz.html

Many historians consider the Battle of Austerlitz Napoleon's most smashing military victory. This Web page contains an overview and several detailed descriptions of the battle. It also presents pictures of the uniforms worn by French, Russian, Prussian, and Austrian soldiers and articles on the traditions and legacies of Napoleon's victory at Austerlitz.

Bulgarian History and Politics

http://asudesign.eas.asu.edu/places/Bulgaria/ref/05HIST.html

The Bulgarian History and Politics site contains a bibliography for Bulgarian history from medieval times to the present. Each source listed in the bibliography is described fully, and there are accompanying pictures.

The Czech Republic: An Introduction

http://www.bsf.cz/project/histgeo.htm

This site mixes geography, geology, and history in a multimedia presentation.

Estonian History

http://www.ibs.ee/history/index.html

Estonian History provides a discussion of Estonia during the period of Soviet control (including a piece on guerrilla groups between 1945 and 1955) and general information on the Baltics.

Eurodocs

http://library.byu.edu/~rdh/eurodocs/

This is Brigham Young University's excellent collection of on-line primary historical documents from Western Europe, including selected transcriptions, facsimiles, and translations. The entries cover political, economic, social, and cultural history.

European Military Uniforms of the Early 19th Century

http://www.nypl.org/research/chss/subguides/milhist/eurocost.html

This Web site contains full-color reproductions of contemporary art that depicts military uniforms from the nineteenth-century British, Austrian, Danish, Dutch, French, Greek, Italian, Prussian, Russian, and Spanish armies.

Historical Atlas of Europe

http://www.ma.org/maps/map.html

This historical atlas of Europe contains dozens of maps arranged by period.

History of European Prints and Printmaking

http://rubens.anu.edu.au/database.html

This site traces the history of European printmaking and includes scanned images of more than 2,800 prints from various countries and periods.

Macedonia History and Politics

http://vislab-www.nps.navy.mil/~fapapoul/macedonia/macedon.html

This site contains a historical survey of Macedonia's long and varied history. From the glories of ancient Greece to the problems of the modern Balkans, this site examines the culture and events of the region.

Polish Home Page

http://info.fuw.edu.pl/poland.html

This site catalogs hundreds of WWW pages in Poland, many relating to history.

Royal Genealogical Data

http://www.dcs.hull.ac.uk/public/genealogy/royal/catalog.html

Royal Genealogical Data is a searchable database on European royalty from ancient times to the present.

WESSWeb

http://www.lib.virginia.edu/wess/

The WESSWeb site aims to provide specialists in Western European studies with professional information and data about ongoing and recent Western European research efforts.

Great Britain and Ireland

Anglo-Saxon Britain

http://www.fas.harvard.edu/~layher1/medscan.html

The Anglo-Saxon Britain pages offer a great deal of information on medieval Scandinavia and Britain. The information is organized by subject, including literature, culture, and history. One can learn about runes, authors, library catalogs, fonts, texts, and more.

The Complete Works of William Shakespeare

http://the@tech.mit.edu/Shakespeare/works.html

This site contains the complete works of Shakespeare in downloadable and searchable format.

Dalriada Celtic Heritage Society

gopher://leapfrog.almac.co.uk:70/11/scotland

A database of information on Celtic culture, including history, folk-lore, myths, and directories for additional information. Special sections highlight "Ancient Gaelic Medicine and Healing" and the arts of "Spinning, Dyeing, Weaving and Metalworking."

English Civil War

http://jpbooks.com/ecws

This is the home page of the English Civil War Society. It contains reenactment information, a variety of articles, and historical facts about the English Civil War.

English Civil War

http://www.idbsu.edu/courses/hy101/english/01.htm

This site contains a searchable and well-organized collection of articles on the events of the English Civil War.

Gaelic Culture Center

http://www.discribe.ca/world/scotland/culture.html

The Gaelic Culture Center includes articles on Scottish history, reli-gion, mythology, folklore, geography, song, language, literature, High-land games, and recipes, including a knee-weakening recipe for haggis!

Gail Dedrick's Guide to the Monarchs of England and Great Britain

http://www.ingress.com/~gail/

Gail Dedrick's Guide to the Monarchs of England and Great Britain provides an illustrated history of the British monarchy. The project is still under construction, however. Only the first seven monarchs who ruled following the Norman Conquest of 1066 have detailed entries at present.

Great Irish Potato Famine

http://www.infi.net/~cksmith/famine/PotatCom.html

This site contains resources on the potato famine, including song lyrics, poetry, and stories of the famine.

H-Albion

http://h-net2.msu.edu/~albion

Sponsored by H-Net, this is the Web site of the H-Albion discussion list, which focuses on all periods of British history. The site contains information about the discussion list and allows one to subscribe. It also includes calls for papers, conference announcements, bibliographies, book reviews, articles, and links to related sites.

History of the Irish Potato Famine

http://www.infi.net/~cksmith/famine/History.html

This site presents a scholarly history of the Irish famine which also aims to draw attention to the contemporary problem of worldwide hunger.

Hume Archives

http://unix1.utm.edu/departments/phil/hume.html

In addition to the texts of the Scottish philosopher David Hume, this site makes available contemporary and modern reviews and commentaries on Hume's work.

Ireland—Archaeology, Folklore, History

http://www.paddynet.ie/island/

This site includes information on Irish mythology, history, religion, magic, place names, ancient ruins, and folklore.

Ireland History Archives

http://library.ccsu.ctstateu.edu/~history/world_history/archives/archive62.html

The Ireland History Archives give a huge list of Web sites concerning Irish history. This site is part of the Europe History Archives, which is a part of the larger Gateway to World History project. Short descriptions of each site are provided.

Irish History on the Web

http://wwwvms.utexas.edu/~jdana/irehist.html

This site is a large database of links to sites on Irish history, including genealogical sites, a hunger strike commemoration page, famine Web sites, and Irish Republic history sites.

Irish Home Pages

http://www.pitt.edu/~mtcst9/irish/irish.html

A list of links to all things Irish. There is a "virtual pub," the Guinness home page, a virtual tourist guide to Ireland, and dozens of articles on Irish history.

Modernism Timeline

http://weber.u.washington.edu/~eckman/timeline.html

The Modernism Timeline contains an annotated timeline for the period between 1890 and 1940. It stresses English events.

Mutiny on the *HMS Bounty*

http://wavefront.wavefront.com/~pjlareau/bounty1.html

Mutiny on the *HMS Bounty* includes biographical information about each member of the ship's crew, as well as facts about the Polynesian women of Pitcairn Island.

Penny Magazine On-Line

http://www.history.rochester.edu/pennymag/

This site contains digitized copies of *Ten Penny Magazine*.

Project Aldus

http://www.jhu.edu/~english/aldus/aldus.main.html

Project Aldus is an electronic archive for primary and secondary materials relating to the English Renaissance and the early modern period.

Regency Fashions

http://locutus.ucr.edu/~cathy/reg3.html

This Web page presents a number of pictures of various fashions, including morning dresses, court dresses, and indoor and outdoor attire. Some French fashions as well, but mostly British.

Register of Research on Northern Ireland

http://www.ulst.ac.uk/services/library/ni/research/research.htm

This site lists over six hundred Irish research projects begun since 1988 and includes links to those that are on-line.

Romantic Chronology

http://humanitas.ucsb.edu/projects/pack/rom-chrono/chrono.htm

This site offers a guide to the literature, history, and culture of France and Britain from 1785 to 1851.

Scottish Economic History Database, 1550–1780.

http://www.ex.ac.uk/~ajgibson/scotdata/scot_database_home.html

This is a searchable database of Scottish economic information for the years 1550 to 1780, arranged under the following headings: "Crop Yields," "Demographic Data," "Price Series," "Wage Series," and "Weather Statistics."

Social Science Bibliography of Northern Ireland 1945–1983

http://www.ulst.ac.uk/services/library/ni/socsci/nidoc.htm

This bibliography includes links to over six thousand related sites.

Victorian History Overview

http://www.stg.brown.edu/projects/hypertext/landow/victorian/history/histov.html

This site presents a broad range of articles on Victorian Britain. Discussions include social history, the empire and international relations, political history, and economic history.

Victorian Web

http://www.stg.brown.edu/projects/hypertext/landow/victorian/victov.html

The Victorian Web was created by Professor George Landow of Brown University to serve as a resource for his course on Victorian literature. Professor Landow's site has expanded beyond its original intent, however. It now contains many Victorian e-texts and information on Victorian artists, design, history, religion, philosophy, technology, and society.

Views of the Famine

http://www.emory.edu/FAMINE

This project gives a number of articles about the famine from the *Illustrated London News, Punch,* and *Pictorial Times.*

Voice of the Shuttle

http://humanitas.ucsb.edu/shuttle/english.html

The Voice of the Shuttle is an outstanding site for research on English literature from all periods. It is arranged by period chronologically and each section discusses prominent authors, course syllabi, electronic journals, criticism, conferences, and calls for papers.

Welcome to the Island

http://www.paddynet.ie/island/

Welcome to the Island is a hypertext exploration of the history and culture of Ireland. The topics covered include mythology, folklore, history, geological features, explanations of place names, and ancient ruins.

Worldwide Sources of Gaelic Sites in English

http://www.smo.uhi.ac.uk/beurla/other_servers.html

This site is a large list of international Gaelic-related Web sites.

France

ARTFL: American and French Research on the Treasury of the French Language

http://tuna.uchicago.edu

ARTFL contains electronic versions of nearly two thousand texts, which range from classic works of French literature to nonfiction prose to technical writing. The subjects covered include literary criticism, biology, history, economics, and philosophy. The database is presently available only to members of universities who are associated with the ARTFL project, but those with access can perform an impressive variety of intratextual and comparative textual searches.

French Studies Web

http://www.nyu.edu/pages/wessfrench

The French Studies Web site is designed to provide access to scholarly resources in French studies. The geographical coverage includes France and the Francophone regions in Belgium and Switzerland.

GIS and Remote Sensing for Archaeology: Burgundy, France

http://deathstar.rutgers.edu/projects/france/france.html

This innovative site shows how mapping technology and satellite imagery can be used in historical research. It offers an evolving presentation of aerial photography and survey data that reveals long-term interactions between cultures and the physical environment.

H-France World Wide Web Site

http://h-net2.msu.edu/~france

Sponsored by H-France and the Society for French Historical Studies, this site contains a wide range of scholarly and general resources. It includes calls for papers, job and conference announcements, classroom resources, maps, links to other sites, an apartment finder service, various bibliographies, and more.

Louis XIV, King of France

http://129.109.57.188/louisvix.htm

This Web site discusses the reign of Louis XIV. It includes historical articles, a bibliography, and many illustrations.

Napoleon

http://www.ping.be/~ping5895/

Sponsored by the Royal Military Academy of Belgium, this site includes information on Napoleon's papers, articles on such themes as the Hundred Days and Napoleon's marshals, and many excellent links.

Napoleon: An Intimate Account of the Years of Supremacy

http://www.napoleonfirst.com/

An on-line museum of the Napoleonic period as depicted in art. Three hundred images in full color are reproduced, along with two hundred black-and-white images.

Paleolithic Cave Paintings in France

http://www.culture.fr/culture/gvpda-en.htm

This site discusses the paintings and engravings dating from the Paleo-lithic Age that have been found in the caves of southern France. The material is in both French and English and includes excellent images of the cave paintings along with historical descriptions.

Paris Maps

http://www.cc.columbia.edu/imaging/html/paris.html

gopher://gutentag.cc.columbia.edu:70/11/fun/pictures/art-history

Paris Maps houses one hundred full-color historical maps of eigh-teenth- and nineteenth-century Paris.

The Siege and Commune of Paris, 1870–1871

http://www.library.nwu.edu/spec/siege/index.html

This WWW page contains more than 1,200 digitized photographs and images drawn from the Northwestern University Library's Siege and Commune Collection.

Treasures from the Bibliothèque Nationale de France: Creating French Culture

http://lcweb.loc.gov/exhibits/bnf/bnf0001.html

This is an exhibit that traces the relationship between power and cul-ture in France from Charlemagne to Charles de Gaulle by using images from manuscripts and books from the French National Library. The site can be accessed in English or French.

Germany

Database of German Nobility

http://www8.informatik.uni-erlangen.de/html/wwp/wwperson.html

This is a searchable database of German nobility (defined as individuals who were associated with the Holy Roman Empire). It contains biographical information, some portraits, and timelines. It can be searched in English, but the biographies are presently in German.

German History

http://www.urz.uni-heidelberg.de/subject/hd/fak7/hist/c1/de/

This site is part of the Virtual Library History Project. It breaks down history by epoch, subtopic, and region. For each area, it lists various related sites.

German Studies on the Internet

http://www.uncg.edu/~lixlpurc/german.html

German Studies on the Internet provides an index of links to resources in both German and English dealing with German culture, language, international affairs, business, and more.

German Surrender Documents

http://library.byu.edu/~rdh/eurodocs/germ/germsurr.html

This site contains an extensive collection of documents relating to Germany's surrender at the end of World War II.

Germanic Heritage Page

http://ucsu.colorado.edu/~anschutz/germanic.html

The Germanic Heritage Page contains sections on Germanic folklore, runelore, religion, language, and literature.

H-German

http://h-net2.msu.edu/~german/

Sponsored by H-Net, this site is the Web affiliate of the H-German discussion list. The site contains information about the discussion list and allows one to subscribe, but it also includes a great deal of information relating to German history. There are calls for papers, conference announcements, bibliographies, book reviews, articles, and links to related sites.

Habsburg

http://h-net2.msu.edu/~habsweb/

This is the Web site of the Habsburg discussion list. Affiliated with H-Net, this group focuses on the history of the central European Habsburg monarchy and its successor states from 1500 to the present. Their Web pages contain information about the discussion list and allow one to subscribe. They also include calls for papers, conference announcements, bibliographies, book reviews, articles, and links to related sites.

Kassandra Project

http://www.reed.edu/~ccampbel/tkp

The Kassandra Project is dedicated to gathering biographical and historical information on German women who were considered visionaries around 1800.

Nineteenth-Century German Stories

http://www.fln.vcu.edu/menu.html

Beautifully illustrated with original manuscript drawings and etchings, this is a collection of nineteenth-century German stories, many of them from the Brothers Grimm. The texts are provided in the original German with English translations.

Italy

H-Italy

http://h-net2.msu.edu/~italy

Sponsored by H-Net, this is the Web site of the H-Italy discussion list. The site contains information about the discussion list and allows one to subscribe. It also includes calls for papers, conference announcements, bibliographies, book reviews, articles, and links to related sites.

History of Sardinia

http://www.crs4.it/~luigi/SARDEGNA/sardegna.html

This is a hypertext document covering the history, culture, and religion of Sardinia from prehistory to the present.

Italy on the Web

http://www.geocities.com/Athens/1809/indein0.html

Italy on the Web is a large gateway to sites on Italian culture and history.

Windows on Italy

http://www.mi.cnr.it:80/WOI

Windows on Italy presents information on Italian culture from prehistory to the present, including geography, government, maps, social patterns, and culture. The site also includes a number of attractive illustrations.

Russia and Eastern Europe

The Alexander Palace Time Machine

http://www.travelogix.com/emp/batchison/

The Alexander Palace Time Machine takes visitors on a beautiful and exciting tour of the Russian palace that was the residence of the Romanov dynasty. Created by Bob Atchison, the tour takes you through the many stunning rooms of the palace, which were inhabited by Nicholas, Rasputin, and others. Along the way, it informs and educates, presenting many family photographs, biographical sketches, historical background, and other interesting tidbits. From an aesthetic standpoint, this is a model site.

Armenian Research Center

http://www.umd.umich.edu/dept/armenian

This site contains information about the history of Armenia and Karabakh. It also details the present-day struggles of Nagorno-Karabakh.

H-Russia

http://h-net2.msu.edu/~russia

This is the Web site of the H-Russia discussion list. Affiliated with H-Net, this group focuses on Russian history. Their Web pages contain information about the discussion list and allow one to subscribe. They also include calls for papers, conference announcements, bibliographies, book reviews, articles, and links to related sites.

Letters of Wolf Lewkowicz

http://web.mit.edu/maz/wolf

This site houses an extensive collection of letters written by a Polish Jew to his American nephew. The letters appear in Yiddish with English translations. They date from 1922 to 1939 and provide rich insight into Jewish life and culture in prewar Poland.

Modern Russian History

http://darkwing.uoregon.edu/~jeseaman/index.html

This site, supported by the University of Oregon, covers twentieth-century Russia. There is a wealth of information on politics and electoral returns and many links to related material.

REEIWEB: Indiana University Russian East European Institute

http://www.indiana.edu/~reeiweb/

This scholarly site lists employment opportunities, grants, and fellowships, call for papers and conferences. There are also links to many similar sites.

Revelations from the Russian Archives

http://www.ncsa.uiuc.edu/SDG/Experimental/soviet.exhibit/soviet.ar
chive.html

ftp://ftp.loc.gov/pub/exhibit.images/russian.archive.exhibit

Revelations from the Russian Archives contains documents from the
former Soviet Union. The site includes both original-language versions
and English translations for most documents. The exhibit has two sections, the first focusing on domestic Soviet issues, the second dealing
with Soviet-American relations.

A Russia Phototrack

http://www.cs.toronto.edu/~mes/russia/photo.html

This site has digitized maps, photographs, and flags from all areas of
Russia.

Russian and East European Studies

http://www.pitt.edu/~cjp/rees.html

This site is a very well-organized directory of Internet sites relating to
Eastern Europe and Russia. Many of the former Soviet states have
developed their own home pages, and this site offers an excellent way
to take the pulse of activities in parts of the world that are rarely
covered by standard American news services.

Russian History

http://www.bucknell.edu/departments/russian/history.html

A hypertext document covering Russian history from the beginnings of
Russian written history to the present day. Special sections are included for the Vikings in Russia, the Khazars (the only nation to convert as a whole to Judaism), Russian monasteries, and more.

The Russian Revolution

http://www.barnsdle.demon.co.uk/russ/rusrev.html

This site has a collection of quotations, photographs, and maps related
to the Russian Revolution.

Soviet Archives

gopher://gopher.tamu.edu:70/11/.dir/soviet.archives.dir

This Web site contains selected documents recently declassified from the Soviet Archives. The documents date from 1917 through the failed coup attempt in 1991 and include papers from the working files of the Central Committee, the Presidential Archive, and the KGB.

Soviet Studies Research Center

gopher://gopher.nato.int/11/secdef/csrc

The Soviet Studies Research Center (a division of the Conflict Studies Research Center) is a British think tank dedicated to analyzing events in the states of the former Soviet Union. Their Web site contains a number of papers that interpret current and past events. Currently, there are texts on such issues as the crisis in Chechnya, the evolution of military justice, Russian relations with the Middle East, and the problems of economic reform. All the reports are written by analysts affiliated with the Conflict Studies Research Center.

Window-to-Russia

http://www.kiae.su/www/wtr/

According to the release, Window-to-Russia (TM) "is a Moscow-based project by Relcom Corporation, initiated to give the worldwide network community the means of WWW access to the variety of information resources from and about Russia."

Scandinavia

A Bit of Swedish History

http://www.luth.se/luth/present/sweden/history/

This site offers information about the history of Sweden, including sections on the Stone Age, Vikings, Norse mythology, and Swedish traditions.

H-Skand

http://www.hum.ou.dk/projekter/h-skand/index.htm

This is the Web site of the H-Skand discussion list. Affiliated with H-Net, this group focuses on Scandinavian history. Their Web pages contain information about the discussion list and allow one to subscribe. They also include calls for papers, conference announcements, bibliographies, book reviews, articles, and links to related sites.

Nordic Pages

http://www.it-kompetens.se/nordic.html

Nordic Pages is a collection of links to information about culture and society in Nordic countries.

Spain

American Academy of Research Historians of Medieval Spain

http://kuhttp.cc.ukans.edu/kansas/aarhms/mainpage.html

The American Academy of Research Historians of Medieval Spain is an association of historians founded twenty years ago to exchange scholarly resources and ideas. This site includes links to discussion lists, translated documents, a reference area, and membership information for the academy.

Spanish Civil War Archive

http://www.miyazaki-mic.ac.jp/faculty/dward/Anarchist_Archives/span civwar/Spanishcivilwar.html

This site offers a variety of information about the Spanish Civil War. There is an illustrated history, a bibliography, biographical files, and links to other interesting sites.

Spanish History and Culture

http://www.DocuWeb.ca/SiSpain/

This site has articles and links on history, foreign affairs, health, social services, and travel. There is also an image collection and a search engine.

Switzerland

University of California at Berkeley Library
Swiss Collections

http://www.lib.berkeley.edu/Collections/Romance/swisshpg.html

The University of California at Berkeley Library Swiss Collections Web page houses many articles on Swiss history, geography, language, education, and current events. There is also an extensive database of electronic texts and a number of links to related materials.

LATIN AMERICA AND THE CARIBBEAN

Cuba Internet Resources

http://ix.urz.uni-heidelberg.de/~pklee/Cuba/

This is a major collection of links to sites on Cuba. It is an excellent starting point.

Cuban History Archives

http://library.ccsu.ctstateu.edu/~history/world_history/archives/cuba.html

This site discusses topics ranging from Cuba's historic ties with the world to the Cuban economy, from politics to dance. It also contains links to related materials.

Documents on Mexican Politics

http://daisy.uwaterloo.ca/~alopez-o/polind.html

This is a large file of articles relating to current Mexican politics and economics. Most of the articles are of current interest, rather than on historical topics. There are also some Mexican government documents and official documents from Mexican political parties.

H-Latam

http://h-net2.msu.edu/~latam

This is the Web site of the H-Latam discussion list. Supported by H-Net, this group focuses on Latin American history. Their Web pages contain information about the discussion list and allow one to subscribe. They also include calls for papers, conference announcements, bibliographies, book reviews, articles, and links to related sites.

H-Mexico

http://h-net2.msu.edu/~halsted/affiliated.html

This is the Web site of the H-Mexico discussion list. Affiliated with H-Net, this group focuses on Mexican history. Their Web pages contain information about the discussion list and allow one to subscribe. They also include calls for papers, conference announcements, bibliographies, book reviews, articles, and links to related sites.

History of Ideas in Latin America

http://www.ldc.lu.se/~latinam/

This site allows on-line discussion of the history of ideas in Latin America. It gives links to related sites and contains full-text copies of some scholarly works on the subject.

LADARK: The Latin American Development Archive

http://www.jhu.edu/~soc/ladark.html

LADARK contains data sets and other information useful to social scientists who are doing research on Latin American development. The data sets are available in either ASCII format or in an SPSS system file. The SPSS system file may be downloaded for Windows statistical analysis programs. Data sets are currently available for Mexican immigrants in the United States, the adaptation process of Cuban and Haitian refugees, and city populations in Latin America.

MayaPages

http://indy4.fdl.cc.mn.us/~isk/maya/maya.html

The MayaPages contain information on Mayan maps, culture, numbers, and language with links to related materials.

Mexico Index

http://www.trace-sc.com/culture.htm

The Mexico Index presents general links on the history, culture, and society of Mexico.

NORTH AMERICA

General American History

American and British History

http://info.Rutgers.edu/rulib/artshum/amhist.html

This is a well-rounded clearinghouse of information on American and British history. It includes access to historic documents, electronic journals, and history discussion lists.

American Hypertexts

http://xroads.virginia.edu/~HYPER/hypertex.html

American Hypertexts contains a great variety of on-line sources in American history, including *The Federalist Papers,* Alexis de Tocqueville's *Democracy in America,* and several works by Mark Twain.

American Memory

http://rs6.loc.gov/amhome.html

American Memory is a tremendous collection of historical texts and images from the National Digital Library Project of the Library of Congress. The site includes an impressive array of primary and archival documents relating to United States history. There are hundreds of photographs and documents from the National Archives and Library of Congress already on-line, and the number is steadily being increased. The site also includes sound files and early American movies from 1897 to 1916, and all of the resources in the collection can be searched in a variety of ways.

American South Internet Resource Center

http://sunsite.unc.edu/doug_m/pages/south/south.html

This site contains links to a number of different sites on the American South, included here are exhibits, multimedia sources, and information on universities.

American Studies Network

http://www.salsem.ac.at/csacl/ams/home.htm

The American Studies Network is a group of European centers, all of which offer an interdisciplinary approach to American studies. The group networks information and resources and tries to promote the study of America in Europe. Their site contains links to related pages and tells about the organization.

American Studies Web

http://www.georgetown.edu/crossroads/asw/

This site includes links to various resources for American studies on the Web. The areas included are economy and politics, gender and sexuality, region and environment, literature, and legal studies.

American Studies Yellow Pages

http://xroads.virginia.edu/~YP/yp_home.html

The American Studies Yellow Pages give an expansive list of resources by discipline. Those areas include gender, philosophy and religion, and social services. There are also links to other pages as well.

Arctic Dawn

http://web.idirect.com/~hland/sh/title.html

Arctic Dawn presents the diary entries that the explorer Samuel Hearne made as he traveled through the Arctic in 1768. The site will be interesting to teachers, students, and history buffs because of the unique glimpse it provides into the colonial explorer's mind. Hearne's diary contains many revealing remarks about "Esquimaux" and other native inhabitants. It captures the violence of life during the eighteenth century, and it also reveals the mixture of awe and exploitation with which European explorers greeted the New World.

A Chronology of United States Historical Documents

http://www.law.uoknor.edu/ushist.html#ind

Compiled by the Law Center of the University of Oklahoma, this site presents a documentary history of the United States from the Magna Carta to Bill Clinton's 1996 State of the Union Address. The documents in this collection make an excellent teaching resource.

Daguerreian Society Galleries

http://java.austinc.edu:80/dag/

The Daguerreian Society has just begun making many of their nineteenth-century photographs available on-line. As this collection grows, it will become a very useful compilation of images.

1850 and 1880 Public Use Microdata Samples

http://www.hist.umn.edu/~ipums/

The 1850 and 1880 Public Use Microdata Samples contain data drawn from the United States Census, which can be downloaded and electronically manipulated.

The Flag of the United States of America

http://www.icss.com/usflag/

This site is a celebratory effort dedicated to the American flag. It includes copies of the Pledge of Allegiance in multiple languages, a history of the flag, links to related Web sites, an index of patriotic writings, and a great deal of miscellaneous information.

Happy Birthday, America!

http://banzai.neosoft.com/citylink/usa/

Happy Birthday, America! is a patriotic site that discusses the history of the Fourth of July. There are articles, images, and sound files.

The History Buff's Home Page

http://www.serve.com/ephemera/historybuff.html

The History Buff's Home Page contains a large collection of articles on a wide array of topics in American history. The site is not aimed at scholars, but even scholars will find articles worthy of their attention.

H-Labor

http://h-net2.msu.edu/~labor

This is the Web site of the H-Labor discussion list. Supported by H-Net, this group focuses on labor history. Their Web pages contain information about the discussion list and allow one to subscribe. They also include calls for papers, conference announcements, bibliographies, book reviews, articles, and links to related sites.

H-Law

http://h-net2.msu.edu/~law

This is the Web site of the H-Law discussion list. Supported by H-Net, this group focuses on legal and constitutional history. Their Web pages contain information about the discussion list and allow one to subscribe. They also include calls for papers, conference announcements, bibliographies, book reviews, articles, and links to related sites.

H-Local

http://h-net2.msu.edu/~local

This is the Web site of the H-Local discussion list. Supported by H-Net, this group focuses on local and public history. Their Web pages contain information about the discussion list and allow one to subscribe. They also include calls for papers, conference announcements, bibliographies, book reviews, articles, and links to related sites.

H-PCAACA

http://h-net2.msu.edu/~pcaaca

Sponsored by the Popular Culture Association and H-Net, this is the Web site of the H-PCAACA discussion list. The site contains information about the discussion list and allows one to subscribe. It also includes calls for papers, conference announcements, bibliographies, book reviews, articles, and links to related sites.

H-Pol

http://h-net2.msu.edu/~pol

Sponsored by H-Net, this is the Web site of the H-Pol discussion list, which focuses on American political history. The site contains information about the discussion list and allows one to subscribe. It also includes calls for papers, conference announcements, bibliographies, book reviews, articles, and links to related sites.

H-Rural

http://h-net2.msu.edu/~rural

Sponsored by H-Net, this is the Web site of the H-Rural discussion list. The site contains information about the discussion list and allows one to subscribe. It also includes calls for papers, conference announcements, bibliographies, book reviews, articles, and links to related sites.

H-South

http://h-net2.msu.edu/~south

This is the Web site of the H-South discussion list. Affiliated with H-Net, this group focuses on the history of the United States South. Their Web pages contain information about the discussion list and allow one to subscribe. They also include calls for papers, conference announcements, bibliographies, book reviews, articles, and links to related sites.

H-West

http://h-net2.msu.edu/~west

This is the Web site of the H-West discussion list. Affiliated with H-Net, this group focuses on the history of the North American West. Their Web pages contain information about the discussion list and allow one to subscribe. They also include calls for papers, conference announcements, bibliographies, book reviews, articles, and links to related sites.

Inaugural Addresses of the Presidents of the United States

http://www.columbia.edu/acis/bartleby/inaugural/index.html

This site contains all the presidential inaugural addresses from Washington to Clinton.

Kidder-Smith Images Project

http://nimrod.mit.edu/rvc/kidder/kiddhome.html

The Kidder-Smith Images Project is a searchable archive of 3,400 slides which document ten centuries of architectural history, mostly American.

Lady Liberty: The Changing Face of American Freedom

http://darwin.clas.Virginia.EDU/~lgg2q/ladyliberty.html

This site looks at the story of Lady Liberty, focusing on the statue, similar monuments, and related iconography. Lady Liberty is an excellent multimedia site.

Migration to America

http://www.turner.com/tesi/html/migration.html

This site aims to show how immigration and ethnic diversity have changed America. It includes a rich teacher's resource guide.

National Trust for Historic Preservation

http://web.nthp.org/index.html

The National Trust for Historic Preservation Web pages include information about places that have been registered as National Historic Landmarks. The pages also contain photographs, place histories, information on the society, and suggestions for visitors.

Naval Historical Center

http://www.history.navy.mil

This is the on-line site of the Naval Historical Center in Washington, D.C. It is presently under construction, but will eventually provide a multimedia account of the United States Navy's long history.

The Oral Argument Page

http://oyez.at.nwu.edu/oyez.html

The Oral Argument Page takes visitors into the chambers of the United State Supreme Court. Jerry Goldman, a professor of political science at Northwestern University, has taken taped court proceedings from the National Archives and made them accessible on Internet. This is an excellent resource for scholars, students, and anyone curious about the workings of the Supreme Court.

From Revolution to Reconstruction

http://grid.let.rug.nl/~welling/usa/

From Revolution to Reconstruction is a multimedia textbook being assembled on-line by students and professors at the University of Groningen. Many of the articles and images were produced by the students or their teachers, but there is also a large collection of solicited essays on a wide range of topics. This is an interesting and creative approach to early American history.

Smithsonian Institution Photographic Services

http://photo2.si.edu/

This page provides access to catalogs of the Smithsonian's image collection, information about ordering images, details on making permission requests, and announcements of upcoming exhibits.

This Week in United States History

http://www.dareware.com/history.htm

This Week in United States History notes important events and birthdates for each day of the present week.

Time-Life Photo Gallery

http://www.pathfinder.com/@@zjkS*mBwsgEAQKEd/pathfinder/photo/sighthome.html

The Time-Life Photo Gallery is an on-line sample of Time-Life's massive photo archives. The number of images that can be accessed is steadily expanding, and the selection on-line at any given time is changed occasionally so that the site operates like an evolving exhibition of Americana.

United States Historical Documents

gopher://wiretap.spies.com/11/Gov/US-History

This site presents gopher links to a great number of historical documents. Among those presented are some of *The Federalist Papers,* the 1775 Declaration of Arms, the Monroe Doctrine, materials on the 1960 U–2 downing, and the two surrender declarations that ended World War II.

United States History On-Line Project

http://solar.rtd.utk.edu/~winslow/

The United States History On-Line Project is still under construction, but the basic outline of what will be added can already be seen. This includes a timeline of United States history, addresses by many of the presidents, and links to similar sites.

United States House of Representatives
Internet Law Library

http://law.house.gov/1.htm

This site includes the latest budget, the *Code of Federal Regulations,* excerpts from the *Congressional Record,* texts of treaties, and international law documents.

African-American History

A–Z of African Studies on the Internet

http://www.zeta.org.au/~johnl/plimb.htm

A–Z of African Studies on the Internet is another general clearinghouse of links to African and African-American sites.

African-American Archives and Images International

http://www.archimag.com/

This site contains a searchable archive of texts and images chronicling African-American history.

African-American History and Literature:
On-Line Texts Directory

http://www.keele.ac.uk/depts/as/Literature/amlit.black.html

This on-line directory contains a large list of links to African-American literature and texts organized by subject, author, and other options.

African-American History Index

http://www.msstate.edu/Archives/History/USA/Afro-Amer/afro.html

The African-American History Index created at Mississippi State University contains a variety of links to resources concerning African-Americans.

African-American Leaders: The Black History Database

http://www.ai.mit.edu/~isbell/HFh/black/bhist.html

Created and maintained at MIT, this index provides brief histories of many important figures and events in African-American history along with links to sites that treat them in more detail.

African-American Mosaic

http://www.vmedia.com/books/www2/data/sec3/subsec3/list11.htm

The African-American Mosaic covers five hundred years of African-American experiences in America. The site includes photographs, etchings, and recordings. The primary focus is on four areas: "Colonization," "Abolition," "Migration," and "The Works Progress Administration." This is also a first-rate site for original source materials.

African-American Resources

http://www.sas.upenn.edu/African_Studies/K-12/menu_EduAFAM.html

Sponsored by the University of Pennsylvania, this site provides links to many scholarly and general resources devoted to African-American history and culture.

African-American Sources

http://http2.sils.umich.edu/HCHS/Afroam/Afroam_sources.html

This site sponsored by the University of Michigan offers links to many scholarly and general resources devoted to African-American history and culture.

African-American Warriors

http://www.abest.com/~cklose/aawar.htm

African-American Warriors provides links to various sites on African-American soldiers in the U.S. armed forces. Among those included are the Buffalo Soldiers, the USCTs, the Tuskegee Airmen, and Colin Powell.

AFROLinks Afrocentric Guide to the World Wide Web

http://www.netlinks.net/Netlinks/AFRO.HTML

This is a large, well-organized guide to dozens of African and African-American sites on the WWW.

Archives of African-American Music and Culture

http://www.indiana.edu/~aaamc/index.html

This is a large database dedicated to all aspects of African-American music and culture, including many links to related sites.

A Deeper Shade of Black

http://www.ai.mit.edu/~isbell/HFh/black/bhcal-toc.html

A Deeper Shade of Black discusses African-American history, film, and literature.

Faces of Science: African-Americans in the Sciences

http://www.lib.lsu.edu/lib/chem/display/faces.html

Faces of Science looks at the past, present, and future of African-Americans in the sciences. It presents biographies of famous African-Americans grouped into scientific discipline, examines the percentages of Ph.D.s granted to African-Americans in each area of the sciences, and contains links to other related sites.

Isis: OurStory

http://www.netdiva.com/ourstory.html

Isis: OurStory is a database dedicated to chronicling the lives of African-American women, from the famous to everyday heroines.

Malcolm X Page

http://www.unix-ag.uni-kl.de/~moritz/malcolm

This Web page presents a variety of information about Malcolm. It includes an interview of Malcolm X by Alex Haley, poems, essays, his funeral eulogy, and links to related sites.

Martin Luther King, "I Have a Dream"

gopher://gopher.vt.edu:10010/02/111/1

This site traces the life of the slain civil rights leader. It has audiofiles of his most memorable speeches, portraits, and links to many sites dedicated to Martin Luther King Jr.

Museum of Slavery in the Atlantic

http://squash.la.psu.edu/~plarson/smuseum/homepage.html

The Museum of Slavery in the Atlantic is designed to provide accurate, engaging, and provocative information to the public about the history of slavery. It includes essays on the history of the slave trade, statistical information, FAQs, and a list of children's books with slavery themes.

National Civil Rights Museum

http://www.mecca.org/~crights/ncrm.html

This site discusses the National Civil Rights Museum in Memphis, Tennessee. It contains a "virtual tour" of the museum's exhibits and their aims. Color and black-and-white photos are included. In addition to the tour, there are links to related sites, and information on membership and admission.

Negro Leagues Baseball On-Line Archives

http://www.infinet/~moxie/nlb/nlb.html

This Web page includes a great deal of information on the history of the Negro Leagues, including team histories and player profiles.

Northeastern African-American Studies

http://www.neu.edu/uc/catalog/AFR.html

Sponsored by Northeastern University, this site presents a number of scholarly and general resources for anyone interested in African-American history. It has a multimedia format and many excellent links.

Persistence of the Spirit

http://www.aristotle.net/persistence/

This site presents an interpretive study of the African-American experience in Arkansas. Included in this site are historical narratives, a photo scrapbook, references, resources, and links to related sites. Good graphics also accompany the material.

Photographic Center of Harlem: Six Decades of Photographs by Austin Hansen

http://pathfinder.com/@@t*lpKvH3PgAAQBmO/pathfinder/features/blackhistory/photo.html

The Photographic Center of Harlem is a massive database of on-line photographs scanned from the works of Austin Hansen.

Ragtime—A History

http://studwww.rug.ac.be/~hvernaev/ragtime/

This is a fun and interesting look at the history of ragtime, including sound clips from a number of pieces.

Slavery Resources On-Line

http://vi.uh.edu/pages/mintz/gilder.htm

Slavery Resources On-Line offers links to slave narratives, Works Progress Administration life histories, and slavery bibliographies.

Still Going On: An Exhibit Celebrating the Life and Times of William Grant Still

http://scriptorium.lib.duke.edu/sgo/start.html

This exhibit explores the life, music, and times of William Grant Still (1895–1978), an African-American composer of both popular and concert music. The exhibit includes biographical information about Still and other noted contemporaries, photographs, and sound clips of his music.

Third Person, First Person: Slave Voices from the Special Collections Library

http://scriptorium.lib.duke.edu/slavery/

Third Person, First Person probes the life experiences of African-American slaves from the late eighteenth century through the nineteenth century, and it examines the enterprise of recovering and preserving the African-American history of the period. The exhibit showcases the kinds of rare materials that under scrutiny reveal the ambitions, motivations, and struggles of people often presumed mute. At present, the site includes scanned documents of letters, posters, bills of sale, and more.

Universal Black Pages: History

http://www.gatech.edu/bgsa/blackpages/history.html

The Universal Black Pages is a large clearinghouse site devoted to collecting information and links relating to African-American issues. This address takes you to the history section of the Black Pages project, which is presently under construction. Plans for the site are ambitious.

University of Michigan Center for Afroamerican and African Studies

http://www.umich.edu/~iinet/caas/

This site has many scholarly resources and links to African-American and African Studies pages.

University of Texas Center for African-American and African Studies

http://www.utexas.edu/depts/caaas/

Another excellent site for scholars or people generally interested in African-American history. This Web page features texts, images, links, and a wide variety of miscellaneous information.

Voices of the Civil Rights Era

http://www.webcorp.com/civilrights/index.htm

Voices of the Civil Rights Era is an audio archive containing different views of the future from Malcolm X, Martin Luther King Jr., John F. Kennedy, and others.

Writing Black USA

http://www.keele.ac.uk/depts/as/Literature/amlit.black.html

Writing Black USA contains full-text essays, books and poems documenting the African-American experience in the United States from colonial times to the present.

Asian-American History

Asian-American Resource Listing

http://www.gi.net/NET/PM-1995/95-11/95-11-27/0013.html

This page is a general clearinghouse of links to pages dedicated to Asian-American culture.

Asian-American Resources

http://www.mit.edu:8001/afs/athena.mit.edu/user/i/r/irie/www/aar.html

This page, sponsored by MIT, contains many links to Asian-American resources on-line. A good starting point.

Documenting Asian-American Literature

http://www.usc.edu/Library/Ref/Ethnic/asian_amer_doc.html

Dedicated to chronicling the contributions of Asian immigrants to American literature, this multimedia site presents text excerpts, a database, and links to other related sites.

Japanese-American Women

http://www.lafayette.edu/faccipop/tomie.htm

Still under construction, this site plans to look at the lives and history of Japanese-American women from a variety of perspectives.

Japanese-Americans Interned in Arkansas—A Short Guide

http://cavern.uark.edu/libinfo/speccoll/shortguides/japanese.html

This site presents a brief history and discussion of American internment practices during World War II.

Korean-American Museum of Art and Culture

http://koma.org/lobby.html

This site is an on-line gallery of exhibitions dedicated to the history and culture of Korean-Americans.

Native American History

California Indian Library Collections

http://www.mip.berkeley.edu/cilc/brochure/brochure.html

Sponsored by the California Indian Library Collections, this site aims to return many artifacts to Indian owners. There are tribal biographies, interactive multimedia collections, and bibliographies.

Cherokee History and Images

http://www.phoenix.net/~martikw/default.html

Cherokee Images is a large photographic database dedicated to preserving the heritage of the Cherokees through images. Most images contain historical annotations.

Historical Images of the Native American Experience

http://www.csulb.edu/gc/libarts/am-indian/nae/

This site presents scanned images documenting the Native American experience from 1600 to the present. The collection includes photographs, etchings, maps, and newsletters.

History of Tecumseh and Tippecanoe

http://www.tippecanoe.com/tec_hist.htm

This Web page gives the history of Tecumseh and the battle of Tippecanoe.

Humboldt State University Native American Directory

http://sorrel.humboldt.edu/~nasp/

Sponsored by Humboldt State University, this site provides links to many sites relating to Native American history.

Indigenous Peoples Archive: NativeWeb

http://web.maxwell.syr.edu/nativeweb/

gopher://marvel.loc.gov:70/11/global/socsci/area/native

NativeWeb includes links to bulletin boards, journals, and articles as well as a searchable database of poetry, stories, prayers, and documents about Native Americans.

Mohican Indian Page

http://www.rpi.edu/~winchd/mohicans.html

This site provides a brief, but growing, account of Mohican culture and history.

Native American Documents Project

http://www.csusm.edu/projects/nadp/nadp.htm

This is an ambitious attempt to put on-line all of the documents that exist concerning Native Americans and their relations with the United States government. The data that currently exists is in three groups— "Published Reports of the Commissioner for Indian Affairs for 1871," "An Allotment Data Collection," and a set of documents entitled "Rogue River War–Siletz Reservation Collection." All documents contain explanatory material, and a short overview of Native American history is provided along with links to related sites.

Native American History Archives

http://library.ccsu.ctstateu.edu/~history/world_history/archives/archive 47.html

This site contains a broad collection of information on many Native American tribes and links to sites dedicated to them.

Native American Resources on the Internet

http://hanksville.phast.umass.edu/misc/NAresources.html

Native American Resources on the Internet is a comprehensive listing of Native American sites, with a well-developed section of historical resources.

Northwest Coast Indian History

http://www.hallman.org/~bruce/indian/history.html

This site plans to provide a collection of historical information about the Indian tribes that resided in the northwestern corner of the United States.

United States Laws Relating to Indian Nations and Tribes

http://law.house.gov/31.htm

This site contains historical texts and legal codes pertaining to Native Americans, as well as electronic versions of current Indian constitutions and laws.

American Women's Studies

American Studies Web: Gender and Sexuality

http://www.georgetown.edu/crossroads/asw

This site provides links to more than fifty sites treating women's concerns as well as gay, lesbian, and bisexual issues.

Feminist Majority Foundation

http://www.feminist.org/

The Feminist Majority Foundation site provides information on current events, a bibliography, and a photographic collection.

Lesbian Herstory Project

http://www-lib.usc.edu/~retter/main.html

The Lesbian Herstory Project is ambitiously attempting to record the stories of lesbians all around the world. It includes the objectives of the project, a list of lesbians, information on lesbians of color, archives, oral histories, books, bibliographies, interviews, and links to related sites.

Multimedia Exhibits: Women's History

http://frank.mtsu.edu/~kmiddlet/history/women/wom-mm.html

Created by Professor Kenneth Middleton of Middle Tennessee State University, this site contains links to various multimedia exhibits on women's history such as PBS specials, press sites, and voice libraries.

National Women's History Project

http://www.nwhp.org/

This site discusses many aspects of women's history, contains famous quotes, and lists upcoming conferences and exhibits dedicated to women's history.

One Woman, One Vote

http://www.pbs.org/learning/k12/resources/one_woman.html

This site served as an on-line companion to a 1995 PBS special on the history of the women's suffrage movement. The site contains a detailed history by Marjorie Wheeler, images, sounds, and a timeline.

Women at War

http://wwwsun.redstone.army.mil/history/women.html

The Women at War site details the work of women at the Redstone military arsenal in Alabama during World War II. It includes very detailed articles with pictures and letters.

Women Writers in English, 1330–1830

http://www.stg.brown.edu/projects/wwp/wwp_home.html

The mission of the Brown University Women Writers Project is to create, develop, and make accessible a state-of-the-art electronic text collection of women's writings in English from roughly 1330 to 1830. The project is intended to support a wide range of activities, including new research on texts and cultural history, publications, and innovative approaches to teaching.

Women's Studies

http://www.middlebury.edu/~lib/women.html

Supported by Middlebury College, this site catalogs links to Web sites on women's issues and lists the women's studies materials in the Middlebury library collections.

Women's Studies Resources

http://www.inform.umd.edu:8080/EdRes/Topic/WomensStudies

Created by the Women's Studies Department of the University of Maryland at College Park, this site lists information on calls for papers, conferences, gender issues, and syllabi for women's studies classes taught all around the country. A picture gallery, government documents collection, and employment listing are also provided.

Women's Suffrage

http://www.history.rochester.edu/class/suffrage/home.htm

This site gives a brief summary of the suffragists and their opponents. It also presents information about Susan B. Anthony, Elizabeth Cady Stanton, the Seneca Falls Convention, and the antisuffragists.

Colonial American History

Collection of Colonial and Early American Currencies

http://www.nd.edu/~rarebook/coins/coin.intro.html

This Web site contains color photographs of coins and bills arranged by the colony or state in which they circulated.

Columbus and the Age of Discovery

http://www.millersv.edu/~Columbus

gopher://marauder.millersv.edu/11/otherMU/Columbus/data/

This site offers a text retrieval system that can access over one thousand text articles from various magazines, journals, newspapers, speeches, and other sources relating to Columbus and the fifteenth and sixteenth centuries.

1492: An Ongoing Voyage

http://sunsite.unc.edu/expo/1492.exhibit/Intro.html

ftp://ftp.loc.gov/pub/exhibit.images/1492.exhibit/

1492: An Ongoing Voyage is an electronic exhibit of the Library of Congress. The site weaves images and text to explore what life was like in pre- and post-Columbian Europe, Africa, and the Americas. The site examines the effect that the discovery of America had on each continent, and the dark elements of colonization are stressed. There are excellent maps, documents, artwork, and supporting text.

Hawaii: Past, Present, Culture, and Myths

http://hawaii-shopping.com/~sammonet/hrlhome.html

This site offers articles on the migrations of the earliest Hawaiians, their gods, myths, and culture. It also has a lot of information about the history and genealogy of Hawaii's royal family. The site includes photographs, etchings, and paintings of early Hawaii.

Ieahcnet

http://h-net2.msu.edu/~ieahcweb

This is the Web site of the Ieahcnet discussion list. Affiliated with H-Net, this group focuses on Colonial and early American history. Their Web pages contain information about the discussion list and allow one to subscribe. They also include calls for papers, conference announcements, bibliographies, book reviews, articles, and links to related sites.

Jamestown Rediscovery Project

http://www.widomaker.com/~apva/

The Jamestown Rediscovery Project is a ten-year comprehensive excavation of Jamestown that began in 1994. This site gives photographs and progress reports on the project to date, as well as plans for the future.

1755: The French and Indian War Home Page

http://web.syr.edu/~laroux/

Created by Larry Laroux, a professional writer, this site serves as a prologue to Laroux's forthcoming book *White Coats,* which will examine the soldiers who fought in the French and Indian War of 1755. The site is presently under construction, but Laroux eventually aims to include histories of important battles, a list of French soldiers who fought in the war, and other statistical records. The site already contains a brief narrative account of the war along with some interesting information and trivia.

Walking Tour of Plymouth Plantation

http://spirit.lib.uconn.edu/ArchNet/Topical/Historic/Plimoth/Plimoth.html

This site includes photographs and a narrative description of the living museum at Plymouth Plantation. It addresses many different aspects of early seventeenth-century life in New England, such as housing, cooking, clothing, and tools.

Revolutionary American History

Ask Thomas Jefferson

http://www.mit.edu:8001/activities/libertarians/ask-thomas-jefferson/
jefferson.html

This site asks a range of questions on topics such as gun control, lust, rebellion, Napoleon, and Puritanism. The site then has links to on-line writings of Thomas Jefferson that address the topic.

Benjamin Franklin: Collected Works

gopher://gopher.vt.edu:10010/11/85

This site provides full-text access to a number of Benjamin Franklin's works.

Benjamin Franklin: Glimpses of the Man

http://sln.fi.edu/franklin/rotten.html

This site contains a short biographical movie and overview of Benjamin Franklin's contributions to science, technology, and politics.

Brigades of the American Revolution

http://csbh.gbn.net/~brigade/barmain.html

The Brigades of the American Revolution is a fascinating page that is still being developed. Eventually, it will provide information on more than 130 Revolutionary units. It lists and breaks down the units in various ways, including by nationality, and it provides links to units with their own home pages.

George Washington Art Project

http://www.columbia.edu/~gmr3/George.html

The George Washington Art Project contains a number of different pictures of America's first president.

H-Shear

http://h-net2.msu.edu/~halstead/affiliated.html

This is the Web site of the H-Shear discussion list. Affiliated with H-Net, this group focuses on early American history. Their Web pages contain information about the discussion list and allow one to subscribe. They also include calls for papers, conference announcements, bibliographies, book reviews, articles, and links to related sites.

Michael D. Meals' Revolutionary War Links Page

http://q.continuum.net/~histnact/revwar/revwar.html

Michael Meals' Revolutionary War page includes information on dozens of Revolutionary Web pages and links to those sites.

Mount Vernon

http://www.mountvernon.org/

This is the official site of Mount Vernon. It offers a virtual tour of Washington's home, including the master bedroom, the grounds, his tomb, and the slave memorial. Commentary on the rooms is included, and the site discusses much of Washington's life through the tour.

Papers of George Washington

http://www.virginia.edu/~gwpapers/

This site is an archive of Washingtonian papers. Many papers are available on-line and information is given on the efforts to publish a comprehensive eighty-five-volume collection of all his writings.

RevWeb

http://www.ccs.neu.edu/home/bcortez/revwar/revwar.html

RevWeb attempts to list all the organizations that are connected with Revolutionary War re-enactments and give links to each. It allows the creation of a home page for similar organizations and allows on-line registration.

Sons of the American Revolution

http://www.sar.org/

This organization and its home page aim to keep the memory of the American Revolution alive. It gives links to on-line versions of the Bill of Rights, the Constitution, and other important historical documents.

Early United States History

The Adventures of Wells Fargo

http://wellsfargo.com/ftr/ftrsty/

The Adventures of Wells Fargo presents several stories taken from the archives of Wells Fargo. The tales capture all the color and excitement of Wells Fargo and the early Wild West.

The Alamo

http://www.dcci.com/San_Antonio/alamo.html

This site gives a very brief history of the Alamo and of the museum there. The museum's hours of operation and location are also explained.

The Alamo

http://numedia.tddc.net/sa/alamo/

This site presents a celebratory look at the battle for the independence of Texas which stresses the Alamo. It offers links to other sites and argues that without this battle, the westward expansion of the United States would have been halted.

Archiving Early America

http://earlyamerica.com/index.html

Archiving Early America presents a history of the young United States by reprinting original documents that were carried in early American newspapers and magazines. One can read documents such as Washington's inaugural address as they appeared to early American readers. This site is a very good resource for teachers, students, and lovers of history.

Diary from the Gold Rush

http://uts.cc.utexas.edu/~scring/index.html

This is the full text of an 1849 diary of a gold prospector who traveled from New York through South America and on to California. The diary also recounts his experiences in the Sacramento Flood of 1850 and the effects of cholera in southern Mexico.

The Federalist Papers

http://www.law.uoknor.edu/hist/federalist.html

This site contains selections from *The Federalist Papers*.

Gallery of the Open Frontier

http://www.unl.edu/UP/gof/home.htm

The Gallery of the Open Frontier is an image collection that will eventually recreate the American frontier through art. Twelve thousand images are planned and historical descriptions will accompany each image.

Native Americans and Early Settlers in California

http://redwoods.com/~ebarnett/natives.html

This site catalogs dozens of early newspaper essays and articles that document the Colonial relations between Native Americans and the settlers.

The Oregon Trail

http://www.isu.edu/~trinmich/Oregontrail.html

Produced by two documentary filmmakers, this site contains a variety of "fantastic facts" that they were unable to include in their documentary on the Oregon Trail.

Originals of Early American Documents

http://www.law.emory.edu/FEDERAL/conpict.html#const

This site contains scanned images of many early American documents, such as the Constitution, the Bill of Rights, and the Declaration of Independence.

Remember the Alamo

http://www.ansaldo.it/~paesani/alamo.html

Remember the Alamo is a very celebratory look at the Alamo siege. The site provides links to a description of the siege and a list of those who died.

The Shooting Iron

http://www.off-road.com/4x4web/si/si.html

The Shooting Iron is dedicated to the history of nineteenth-century guns, gunsmiths, and marksmanship.

Temple of Liberty: Building the Capitol for a New Nation

http://lcweb.loc.gov/exhibits/us.capitol/s0.html

The Temple of Liberty is an impressive multimedia exhibit drawn from the holdings of the Library of Congress. The exhibit shows the various plans which were considered for the new capitol of the United States, and it discusses the history surrounding each plan's success or failure.

Washington's Farewell Address, 1796

gopher://wiretap.spies.com/00/Gov/US-Speech/washing.fw

This site gives the text of Washington's farewell address.

The Civil War

African-American Civil War Memorial

http://www.cr.nps.gov/itd/dcmem.html

This page presents details on the planned African-American Civil War Memorial, including location, design, and a brief history of the monument. It also gives links to related pages.

American Civil War

http://funnelweb.utcc.utk.edu/~hoemann/cwarhp.html

The American Civil War page attempts to gather in one location the best electronic files on the Civil War and provide links to them. The site contains many resources, including diaries, speeches, and letters.

American Civil War—Documents and Books

http://www.access.digex.net/~bdboyle/docs.html

This site includes a number of contemporary letters, diaries, and other documents relating to the Civil War.

American Civil War Home Page

http://cobweb.utcc.utk.edu/~hoemann/cwarhp.html

The American Civil War Home Page is a good clearinghouse of Civil War information. It presents Civil War letters, diaries, battle information, photographs, and miscellaneous military information.

The Battlefield Web

http://www.ahoynet.com/battlefield/battlefield.html

Created by AHOYnet, this site presents photographs of the Virginia campaigns.

CAMP CHASE GAZETTE

http://nemesis.cybergate.net/~civilwar/

The *Camp Chase Gazette* is a cyberspace journal for those interested in Civil War reenactments. In addition to providing everything you wanted to know (and probably more) about getting into the activity, the site has many articles on the Civil War. It also includes links to other Web pages, on-line subscription procedures, and information on buying Civil War equipment.

Camp Moore Confederate Cemetery and Museum

http://ourworld.compuserve.com/homepages/forrest64/

This site describes the cemetery and museum at Camp Moore.

Civil War Information, Documents, and Archive

http://www.access.digex.net/~bdboyle/cw.html

This site provides links to a number of different sources and archives. It also includes map archives, regimental histories, and information about Civil War parks. It also contains orders of battle and e-text versions of works such as *The Life of Frederick Douglass.*

Civil War Letters of Galutia York

http://exlibris.colgate.edu/gyork/gyork1st.html

Created by the Colgate College Library, this site contains more than fifty Civil War letters written by the oldest son of a New York farming family.

Civil War Photograph Gallery

http://www.socomm.net/~civilwar

The Civil War Photograph Gallery is a large and growing collection of images capturing every facet of the war.

Civil War Photographs Home Page

http://rs6.loc.gov/cwphome.html

This large site provides on-line access to more than one thousand photos contained in the Library of Congress's Civil War collection, and the number of on-line images is growing.

Civil War Poetry and Music

http://www.erols.com/kfraser/

This site contains poetry and music from both Union and Confederate figures and gives their historical context.

Civil War Resources on the Internet: Abolitionism to Reconstruction (1830s–1890s)

http://www.rutgers.edu/rulib/artshum/civwar-2.html

Civil War Resources on the Internet offers a subject archive for the American and British History Page maintained at Rutgers University. This site provides access to a wealth of primary sources, including more than one thousand Civil War photographs.

Civil War Sites in the Shenandoah Valley of Virginia

http://www.cr.nps.gov/abpp/svs0-1.html

This site describes the history of fifteen battlefields in the Shenandoah Valley. It also contains information on current attempts to preserve the area.

Civil War Soldiers and Sailors System

http://www.cr.nps.gov/itd/welcome.html

The Civil War Soldiers and Sailors System site is an effort to construct a comprehensive database of information on all those who fought in the Civil War.

Confederate States of America Document Collection

http://www.snider.net/home/color/csadoc.htm

This on-line Civil War collection contains many documents from the Confederate States of America.

Diaries from Pennsylvania and Virginia

http://jefferson.village.virginia.edu/vshadow/diary.html

This site presents selections from six diaries, dating mostly from the Civil War.

Diary of 1861

http://pages.prodigy.com/GA/daddyof3/diary.html

This site presents the diary of a teenage boy who lived on a plantation in Georgia during the Civil War.

Fredericksburg and Spotsylvania National Military Park

http://www.nps.gov/frsp/frspweb.htm

Sponsored by the National Parks Service, this site gives information on the largest military park in the nation. It allows you to preplan your visit and includes information on coming events, park history, and educational opportunities.

Gettysburg Discussion Group

http://www.arthes.com:1030/gettys.html

This site gives information about the Gettysburg discussion group. It allows on-line registration and gives information about the next muster as well as including a number of links to related sites. It also provides one good picture of the fiftieth reunion of the veterans of Gettysburg and a great deal of data about Gettysburg in general, such as a listing of the Union Medal of Honor winners and the order of battle.

H-Civwar

http://h-net2.msu.edu/~civwar

This site is the Web page of the H-Net–sponsored H-Civwar discussion list. The site contains information about the discussion list and allows one to subscribe. It also includes calls for papers, conference announcements, bibliographies, book reviews, articles, and links to related sites.

Illinois in the Civil War

http://www.outfitters.com/illinois/history/civil/

Illinois in the Civil War explores the more than 250,000 Illini who served in the Civil War. It presents complete rosters of some of the units that served, along with references to other works on the subject.

Indiana in the Civil War

http://www.holli.com/~ligget/cw.html

Indiana in the Civil War discusses the 200,000 Hoosiers who served in the Civil War. It lists the members of the Indiana regiments and battles that Indiana troops were involved in. It also contains links to other servers and announcements concerning Indiana and the Civil War.

Letters from an Iowa Soldier in the Civil War

http://www.ucsc.edu/civil-war-letters/home.html

This site houses the letters of Private Newton Robert Smith to his sweetheart and his parents.

Mississippi Civil War Regiments

http://home.teclink.net/~moorerga/cw/cwlist.html

This site contains an enormous amount of information on Mississippi's participation in the Civil War. It includes casualty lists, orders of battle, and links to related Web sites.

Mobile Bay: First Strike for Grant's Strategy

http://www.maf.mobile.al.us/area_history/battle.html

The Mobile Bay site details the 1864 battle that was a strategic victory for the Union, and it explains how the battle helped Lincoln win the 1864 election.

Ohio in the Civil War

http://www.infinet.com/~lstevens/a/civil.html

This site lists the various units that were involved in the Civil War. It also describes musicians who were involved and discusses their war stories.

Researching People of the Civil War Era

http://www.cwc.lsu.edu/other/genealogy/

This is a very useful site for anyone who is just beginning the process of genealogical research, but the site has limited information for those already familiar with the research process.

Selected Civil War Photographs

http://rs6.loc.gov/cwphome.html

Selected Civil War Photographs is a large collection of more than one thousand digitized images that can be searched in several ways. The site also gives information on Matthew Brady and other photographers.

Selected Civil War Photographs from the Library of Congress, 1861–1865

http://lcweb2.loc.gov/cwphome.html

This is a searchable database containing thousands of Civil War photographs. The site enables one to search the collection by topic (such as "hospitals") or by name (such as "William T. Sherman").

Shiloh National Military Park

http://jackson.freenet.org/jfn/axm8419/shiloh.html

This unofficial site provides information about the Battle of Shiloh, the park, and an upcoming reenactment. It also offers links to related sites.

Sons of Union Veterans

http://suvcw.org/

The Sons of Union Veterans site contains a large amount of information about this successor organization to the Grand Army of the Republic. It provides an on-line copy of some issues of *The Banner,* its national magazine, and includes membership information, links to other browsers, and details on similar Confederate organizations.

United States Civil War Center

http://www.cwc.lsu.edu/

The United States Civil War Center is the home page for a center devoted to the preservation and distribution of information relating to the Civil War. The site contains a wide variety of Web links to Civil War sites.

Valley of the Shadow Project

http://jefferson.village.virginia.edu/vshadow2/

Created by Edward Ayers of the University of Virginia, this site is an excellent multimedia resource for students and teachers of the American Civil War. It contains primary documents, images, sounds, and historical discussions.

Virginia Military Institute Archives

http://www.vmi.edu/~archtml/index.html

This site includes interesting manuscripts and records documenting the Virginia Military Institute's heritage and its place in military history. There are more than six thousand photographs and volumes of alumni records.

Restoration and Gilded Age American History

H-Shgape

http://h-net2.msu.edu/~shgape

This is the Web site of the H-Shgape discussion list. Sponsored by the Society of History for the Gilded Age and Progressive Eras and H-Net, this site contains information about the discussion list and allows one to subscribe. It also includes calls for papers, conference announcements, bibliographies, book reviews, articles, and links to related sites.

How the Other Half Lives

http://www.cis.yale.edu/amstud/inforev/riis/title.html

How the Other Half Lives is a hypertext edition of Jacob Riis' classic 1890 book of the same title, which exposed the conditions of life in New York City tenements. The site includes many of the photographs that moved readers of the original book.

Images from the Philippine–United States War

http://www.msstate.edu/Archives/History/USA/filipino/filipino.html

This site contains a variety of photographs that range from the leader of the Philippine insurrection to the Boston office of the Anti-Imperialist League. There is also an extensive collection of editorial cartoons and maps.

Mark Twain on the Philippines

http://web.syr.edu/~fjzwick/

This is Professor Zwick's now famous site containing Mark Twain's satirical criticism of American imperialism in general and American imperialism in the Philippine War of 1899–1902 specifically.

19th-Century Scientific American On-Line

http://www.history.rochester.edu/Scientific_American/

This Web site contains an archive of past issues of *Scientific American* from 1845 to 1859. This is not an official site sponsored by the magazine.

Nineteenth-Century Women Writers Web

http://clever.net/19cwww/

The Nineteenth-Century Women's Writers Web site contains the writings of many literary figures, listings of journals and presses concerned with the topic, and links to other sites of interest.

Victorian Society in America

http://www.burrows.com/vict.html

This society aims to preserve and celebrate the nineteenth-century history of the United States. The society has a membership of three thousand, comprised of historians, museum curators, and art gallery operators. It sponsors symposiums, summer schools, and an annual meeting. Information about all of its activities is available on-line.

The War from a Parlor: The Philippine-American War

http://web.syr.edu/~fjzwick/stereo/index.html

The War from a Parlor presents the conflicting images of the Philippine–American War that were carried by the American media. The site does a good job reproducing the letters, photos, and news stories that shaped American perceptions of the war.

Twentieth-Century American History

American Prohibition Project

http://www.cohums.ohio-state.edu/history/projects/prohibition/

The American Prohibition Project chronicles contemporary reaction to the prohibition movement. The site captures the sentiments for and against prohibition and includes historical analysis.

Anti-Imperialism in the United States, 1898–1935

http://web.syr.edu:80/~fjzwick/ail98-35.html

This site contains full-text primary and secondary materials relating to American anti-imperialism.

Bay of Pigs

http://www.ucs.mun.ca/~mhunter/H2510.TXT

This site offers a brief history of the Bay of Pigs operation. There are also links to other related sites and a bibliography.

Carl Van Vechten Photographs, 1932–1964

http://lcweb2.loc.gov/vvhome.html

This site contains portraits of literary figures, artists, celebrities, and individuals who were prominent from 1932 to 1964.

Collective Memories of the Cuban Missile Crisis

http://www.stg.brown.edu/projects/classes/mc166k/missile_crisis_34. html

This site presents historical recollections of the Cuban Missile Crisis.

Early Motion Pictures, 1897–1916

http://lcweb2.loc.gov/papr/mpixhome.html

Early Motion Pictures, 1897–1916 is a searchable database of very short early motion picture clips. Most clips fall into the following categories: President William McKinley, the Pan-American Exposition of 1901, and San Francisco before and after the Great Earthquake and Fire of 1906.

Ellis Island

http://www.i-channel.com/ellis/index.html

This site includes essays on immigration and the Ellis Island experiences of many immigrants.

FDR Cartoon Collection

http://www.wizvax.net/nisk_hs/departments/social/fdr_html/FDRmain.html

This site is a searchable collection of Franklin D. Roosevelt cartoons.

Gangsters!

http://www.well.com/user/mod79/

Gangsters! contains scholarly and popular information on famous gangsters, crimefighters, wise-guy films, and the gangster way of life.

General Sound Samples

http://web.msu.edu/vincent/general.html

This sound collection includes short sound clips from a variety of famous figures, including Florence Nightingale, Amelia Earhart, Will Rogers, and Isaac Asimov.

Great Earthquake and Fire of 1906

http://www.sfmuseum.org/1906/06.html

This is a very rich source for primary material relating to the 1906 earthquake and fire in San Francisco. The site has a number of eyewitness accounts, police department reports, descriptions of the operations undertaken by the United States Army and Navy during the emergency, reports on the relief and recovery efforts, engineering and scientific assessments, and photographs.

Guide to the Papers of Louis Dembitz Brandeis

http://www.louisville.edu/groups/library-www/law/brandeis.html

Louis Dembitz Brandeis served as an outspoken United States Supreme Court justice from 1916 to 1941. This site contains a biographical sketch of Brandeis and digitized versions of many of his writings.

Historical Statistics on Banking, 1934–1994

gopher://gopher.fdic.gov:70/11/sob/hist94

gopher.sura.net: choose Databases and Network Information/FDIC Gopher

Historical Statistics on Banking covers American banking from 1934 to 1994. The site has statistical information from the Federal Deposit Insurance Corporation on insured banks.

Hot Links on the Cold War

http://www.stmartin.edu/~dprice/cold.war.html

Hot Links on the Cold War contains an excellent list of links to resources on the cold war. It connects users to various agencies including the CIA and the FBI. It also contains primary documents and original observations from the page's author, Daniel Price, who is an anthropologist working on a history of how the cold war affected American anthropology.

Images of My War

http://www.ionet.net/~uheller/vnbktoc.html

Images of My War contains a series of short essays describing one man's experiences in Vietnam.

The John F. Kennedy Assassination Home Page

http://www.informatik.uni-rostock.de/~impetus/Kennedy/index.html

The John F. Kennedy Assassination Home Page recounts the many conspiracy theories surrounding JFK's death. The site also provides links to other sites of interest.

Life History Manuscripts from the Folklore Project, 1936–1940

http://lcweb2.loc.gov/wpaintro/wpahome.html

This site includes interviews from the Federal Writers' Folklore Project, a New Deal program that attempted to record American folktales and the recollections of Americans from many walks of life. The broad topics covered are "African-Americans," "Agriculture," "Immigration," "Labor," "Recreation," and "Women."

New York City History: Lower East Side at the Turn of the Century

http://140.190.128.190:80/SMC/Dept/history/contents.html

New York City History is a collection of contemporary accounts, articles, and documents that examine conditions in turn-of-the-century New York.

95-75

http://www.cc.rochester.edu:80/SBA/95-75/

95-75 celebrates the seventy-five-year history of the women's rights movement in America.

Office of Human Radiation Experiments Home Page

http://www.ohre.doe.gov

The Office of Human Radiation Experiments, which was formed in March 1994, is undertaking the Department of Energy's efforts to tell the agency's cold war story of radiation research using human subjects. This site is part of the OHRE's effort to identify and catalog relevant historical documents from the Department of Energy's immense collection of records which is scattered across the country. The site provides access to recently declassified documents relating to the issue, including scanned images of the actual memos, research proposals, and letters.

Photographs from the Detroit Publishing Company, 1880–1920

http://lcweb2.loc.gov/detroit/dethome.html

This site contains a searchable exhibit of over 25,000 photographs, mostly of the eastern United States. The photos cover all aspects of American life, such as cities and towns, factories, transportation, amusement parks, and recreation. There is also an extensive collection of portraits of well-known Americans of the period.

Prohibition Movement

http://www.cohums.ohio-state.edu/history/projects/prohibition/

This Web page links visitors to a number of Web sites on Prohibition.

San Francisco Digger Archives

http://www.webcom.com/~enoble/diggers/diggers.html

This page traces the history of the art theater troupe that helped launch the hippie phenomenon.

The Sixties

http://www.slip.net/~scmetro/sixties.htm

The Sixties exhibits a large collection of information on the 1960s put together by a broadcaster and editor. The items on-line include Martin Luther King's "I Have a Dream" speech; songs from Peter, Paul, and Mary; the Elvis home page; the Andy Griffith Show Page; and material on the Beatles, with much more coming soon.

The Sixties Project and the Vietnam Generation

http://jefferson.village.virginia.edu/sixties

The Sixties Project catalogs links to bibliographies, discussion groups, syllabi, and other Web sites of interest.

Sound Samples from American Presidents

http://web.msu.edu/vincent/presidents.html

This Web site contains short (two-to-five-minute) sound clips from United States presidents, including clips from Theodore Roosevelt, William H. Taft, Woodrow Wilson, and Bill Clinton. Your computer must have a program that is capable of playing 8 kilohertz ulaw sound files.

State Department Publications and Reports

http://www.state.gov/index.html

This site contains many documents from the State Department. The documents include the Background Note Series, which provides practical information about the climate, culture, and living conditions of every country in the world; country reports on economic conditions and human rights; and reports on global terrorism.

United States Supreme Court Decisions

http://www.law.cornell.edu/supct/supct.table.html

This page offers a searchable database of full-text Supreme Court decisions from 1990 to the present.

Viet Nam Generation: Recent History and Culture

http://jefferson.village.virginia.edu/sixties/HTML_docs/VG_Journal_entry.html

This site offers an interdisciplinary approach to the Vietnam War and its impact on American society and culture. Personal narratives, poetry, and political issues are all available.

Watergate

http://netspace.net.au/~malcolm/wgate.htm

This site discusses in brief the whole litany of Watergate events. It gives background, consequences, and links to related sites. It also discusses the changes in the political landscape due to Watergate.

Wild Bohemians

http://www.halcyon.com/colinp/bohemian.htm

This page contains many links to sites on the hippie and biker movements, Haight-Ashbury, the Beat generation, and groups like the Grateful Dead.

Works Progress Administration Life History Manuscripts

http://rs6.loc.gov/wpaintro/wpahome.html

This is an introduction to the Works Progress Administration Life History Project, a New Deal effort that attempted to capture the life experiences of Americans from all walks of life. The site includes full texts of the 2,900 documents compiled by three hundred interviewers in twenty-four states, and all of the various versions of the projects activities are included so one can see how the project progressed.

Canadian History

Anglicans, Puritans, and Quakers in Seventeenth-Century Newfoundland

http://www.mun.ca/rels/ang/texts/ang1.html

This site contains a collection of essays, documents, and links dealing with religious history in seventeenth-century Newfoundland.

Beaton Institute of Cape Breton Studies

http://eagle.uccb.ns.ca/beaton/texts/document/beaton.html

This site highlights the activities and research of the Beaton Institute. There are also many links to related materials.

British Columbian History

http://www.freenet.victoria.bc.ca/bchistory.html

This is an excellent multimedia site, with an illustrated history of British Columbia, articles, commentaries, and links to related sites.

Building Canada

http://blackader.library.mcgill.ca/cac/bland/building/

Building Canada contains the Blanding Collection of photographic images which focuses on Canadian architectural heritage. The materials are indexed and accompanied by descriptive notes.

Canada's National History Society

http://www.cyberspc.mb.ca/~otmw/cnhs/cnhs.html

This site contains resources on the teaching and preservation of Canadian history.

Canadadisk

http://schoolnet.carleton.ca/cdisk/

Canadadisk is a collection of more than 2,300 photos and images capturing Canadian history.

Canadian Communities, Local History

http://ellesmere.ccm.emr.ca/ourhome/

Canadian Communities, Local History is a general gateway to Canadian local-history sites.

Canadian Heritage

http://www.magi.com/~westdunn/

Using sound clips, videos, photographs, and essays, this site captures Canadian history in a variety of ways.

Canadian History Archives

http://library.ccsu.ctstateu.edu/~history/world_history/archive/archive 46.html

This site contains a variety of materials for teachers and students of Canadian history. There are links to images, essays, movies, sound clips, journals, and other multimedia resources.

Canadian Women in History

http://www.niagara.com/~merrwill/

This Web site provides histories of Canadian women from various walks of life. Some thirty biographies are now available. The site also includes trivia, a woman of the week, and links to related sites.

Champlain: Canadian Information Explorer

http://info.ic.gc.ca/champlain/champlain.html

Champlain is a searchable index of the many Internet sites sponsored by the Canadian government.

H-Canada

http://h-net2.msu.edu/~canada

Sponsored by H-Net, this is the Web site of the H-Canada discussion list. The site contains information about the discussion list and allows one to subscribe. It also includes calls for papers, conference announcements, bibliographies, book reviews, articles, and links to related sites.

HISTORY OF SCIENCE
AND TECHNOLOGY

Astronomy History Links

http://antwrp.gsfc.nasa.gov/htmltest/jbonnell/www/hist.html

Astronomy History Links is a gateway to related sites.

Biographical Dictionary for the History of Science, Technology, and Medicine

http://www.asap.unimelb.edu.au/hstm/hstm_bio.htm

This is an extensive database with entries by well-respected scholars. It can be searched by name or key word.

Biographical Index of Chemists, Biologists, Mathematicians, Physicists, and Psychologists

http://userwww.sfsu.edu/~rsauzier/Biography.html#Philosophy

This site includes ten to thirty biographies for each field, focusing on nineteenth- and twentieth-century figures.

Caltech Archives PhotoNet

http://www.caltech.edu/archives/

The Caltech Archives PhotoNet contains a collection of more than two thousand photos relating to the history of science and technology.

CERN Historical and Scientific Archives

http://wwwas.cern.ch/ASinfo/AS-SI/archives/Welcome.html

This is an excellent database of historical information on the development of computer technologies.

The Cesarean Section: A Brief History

http://www.nlm.nih.gov/exhibition/cesarean/cesarean_1.html

Cesarean sections have been performed since ancient times, and one can find diaries, reports, and other papers recording the experiences of mothers and babies in both Western and non-Western cultures. This exhibit highlights the history of the procedure in different areas of the world. A number of historical etchings and woodcuts accompany the text.

Chemical Engineering History

http://www.cems.umn.edu/~aiche_ug/history/h_time.html

This site presents a basic history of chemical engineering, from 1635 to the present. It also includes links to related sites on chemical engineering.

Electronic Resources in the History of Science, Medicine, and Technology

http://www.welch.jhu.edu/history/IOHMelec.html

This site provides links to a great variety of Web pages dedicated to the history of science, medicine, and technology.

Enter Evolution: History and Theory

http://www.ucmp.berkeley.edu/history/evolution.html

This Web page discusses the history and future of evolutionary thought. It presents numerous historical essays as well as biographies of many figures in science before and after Darwin.

The Hiroshima Project

http://www.khm.uni-koeln.de/~akke/HiroshimaProject/

The Hiroshima Project presents a wealth of information about the atomic bomb. References to literary sources, representations of the bomb in film and the arts, links to related Web pages, and historical sketches are just a sample of this site's contents.

History of Astronomy

http://aibn55.astro.uni-bonn.de:8000/~pbrosche/astoria.html

This Web page houses information on famous astronomers, antique equipment, important discoveries, and more.

History of Australian Science and Technology

http://www.asap.unimelb.edu.au/

This site provides access to a wide variety of resources relating to the history of Australian science and technology.

History of Computing

http://ei.cs.vt.edu/~history/

This site contains photographs and biographical information on prominent computer scientists, reports on historically significant computer labs or experiments, lists of computer history organizations, and access to archival information.

History of Genetics Bibliography

http://pubweb.ucdavis.edu/Documents/hps/Histgen.html

This site presents papers in genetics, including some stretching back to 1865, links to other sites, syllabi, and a reading list.

History of Mathematics

http://www.maths.tcd.ie/pub/HistMath/HistMath.html

Sponsored by the University of Dublin, this site provides a great deal of biographical information and the full texts of some classical works on mathematics.

History of Mathematics Home Page

http://aleph0.clarku.edu/~djoyce/mathhist/mathhist.html

This site presents a variety of resources, including Web pages, on-line journals, regional resources, and chronologies.

History and Philosophy of Science and Technology

http://www.physics.wisc.edu/~shalizi/hyper-weird/history-of-science.html

This site includes a virtual library, Usenet guide, mailing list references, biographies, and a biographical directory.

History of Psychology

http://www.ai.mit.edu/people/deniz/html/node2.html

This page gives a brief history and links to books on the subject by this Web page's author.

History of Science, Medicine, and Technology

http://www.jhu.edu/~phil/relfold/histsci.html#theTop

This site is a well-rounded clearinghouse, developed by Johns Hopkins University, with good annotated listings for pages on all areas of the history of science and technology. A very good starting point for this topic.

History of Science, Technology, and Medicine

http://www.asap.unimelb.edu.au/hstm/hstm_ove.html

Supported by the University of Melbourne, this site has a large selection of resources dealing with scientific organizations, museums, electronic journals, and discussion groups.

The Jesuits and the Sciences

http://www.luc.edu/libraries/science/jesuits/index.html

A remarkable characteristic of the Jesuits during the period of their founding (1540–1773) was their involvement in the sciences. This exhibition is very well illustrated and contains articles and biographical information dealing with this topic.

MacTutor History of Mathematics Archive

http://www-groups.dcs.st-and.ac.uk/~history/index.html

The MacTutor History of Mathematics Archive contains hundreds of biographical sketches of famous mathematicians and essays on the historical development of mathematics.

Mayo Clinic History

http://www.mayo.edu/general/history.html

This is a very general history of the Mayo Clinic with a few pictures and links to other sites.

Nobel Laureates in the Sciences: Medicine

http://www.lib.lsu.edu/sci/chem/guides/srs118_medicine_us.html

This site lists the scholars who have won Nobel Prizes. The site also includes a biography of Alfred Nobel and links to related Web pages.

Nobel Prize Internet Archive

http://www.alma2.com/nobel

The Nobel Prize Internet Archive lists and describes the 1995 Nobel Prize winners. The site contains links to the Nobel foundation and to other related sites.

On-Line Images from the History of Medicine

http://wwwoli.nlm.nih.gov/databases/olihmd/olihmd.html

This is a searchable database of more than 60,000 images (including photographs, artwork, and printed materials) drawn from the National Library of Medicine. It includes photographs of military hospitals, rescue teams, historical medical equipment, and famous doctors from ancient times to the present.

Scientific and Medical Antiques

http://www.duke.edu/~tj/sci.ant.html

ftp://ftp.duke.edudirectory=pub/sci-ant

This site offers information about scientific and medical antiques, including telescopes, microscopes, scales, electrical and magnetic items, surveying equipment, navigation devices, maps, globes, bloodletting devices, and electrotherapy apparatus.

Smithsonian Natural History Home Page

http://nmnhwww.si.edu/nmnhweb.html

The Smithsonian Natural History Home Page includes documents and data about the museum's research and nature collections, which comprise more than 120 million scientific and cultural artifacts from around the world.

United States Patent Citation Database

http://cos.gdb.org/repos/pat/

This database allows one to search for patents in a variety of ways—by name, title, reference number, and classification. There is also a very good on-line help feature.

WWW Sites Relating to the History of Medicine

http://www.tulane.edu/~matas/paths_hist.html

This is a large collection of links focused on medical history.

MILITARY HISTORY AND HOLOCAUST STUDIES

GENERAL MILITARY HISTORY

The American War Library

http://members.aol.com/amerwar

This is an extensive library on war veterans that includes statistics, photos, lists of veterans, and more.

De Re Militari Information Server

http://www.olcommerce.com/cadre/deremil/index.html

De Re Militari contains a wealth of resources on classical and medieval military history.

E-HAWK: Electronic Headquarters for the Acquisition of War Knowledge

http://www.olcommerce.com/cadre/index.html

E-Hawk presents articles and documents on military science, current events, military graphics, and veterans' resources.

H-Minerva

http://h-net2.msu.edu/~minerva

This is the Web site of the H-Minerva discussion list. Supported by H-Net, this group focuses on the history of women's involvement in war and the military. Their Web pages contain information about the discussion list and allow one to subscribe. They also include calls for papers, conference announcements, bibliographies, book reviews, articles, and links to related sites.

H-War

http://h-net2.msu.edu/~war

This is the Web site of the H-War discussion list. Affiliated with H-Net, this group focuses on military history. Their Web pages contain information about the discussion list and allow one to subscribe. They also include calls for papers, conference announcements, bibliographies, book reviews, articles, and links to related sites.

Mil-Hist

http://www.olcommerce.com/cadre/milhist/index.html

This site covers world military history from ancient times to the present day. This is a good starting point for military history.

Militaria Magazine

http://www.militaria.com

Militaria's Web page serves military buffs and historians alike. On-line books, photographs, scholarly articles, and links to other sites are included. There are also indexes of magazines such as *After the Battle, RAIDS,* and *Militaria.*

The Military History Collections of the New York Public Library

http://gopher.nypl.org/admin/../research/chss/subguides/milhist/home.html

The Military History Home Page covers all the major wars that the United States has been involved in, as well as the Spanish Civil War and the Russian Revolution. Special topics covered by the site include military uniforms and regimental histories. The presentations are a mixture of primary and secondary materials with some multimedia links.

United States Army Center of Military History

http://www.army.mil/cmh-pg/

This site contains a data sheet on the center and on army history, full-text listings of Medal of Honor citations, and lists of military books and articles on-line.

War and Military Picture Archive

http://www.vestnett.no/vulcan/pics/picindex.html

The War and Military Picture Archive is a large collection of photographs. The archive includes images of World War I, World War II, Korea, Vietnam, and other conflicts.

WORLD WAR I

The Great War

http://www.pitt.edu/~novosel/ww1.html

The Great War contains a number of poems and literary accounts of World War I, assorted historical sketches, and an excellent list of links to related sites.

Trenches on the Web

http://www.worldwar1.com/

Trenches on the Web is an excellent multimedia site. It contains many articles, images, and sound files. Included in the collection are several of the Willy-Nicky telegrams, a reference library, a timeline, and a search feature.

The Versailles Treaty—1919

http://ac.acusd.edu/History/text/versaillestreaty/vercontents.html

The Versailles Treaty Web site includes the complete text of the 1919 treaty that ended World War I. This site also has a number of contemporary maps, charts, and cartoons relating to the treaty and a chronology of Woodrow Wilson's battle with Congress over the League of Nations.

World War I Document Archive

http://www.lib.byu.edu/~rdh/wwi/

The World War I Document Archive is a project to assemble all of the available documents on World War I. It includes a citation guide and a link to a mailing list. Most documents are European at present, but a few American materials are provided.

World War I Photographs

http://www.amug.org/~avishai/WWI.html

This site contains a number of photographs from a family album.

WORLD WAR II AND THE HOLOCAUST

A-Bomb WWW Museum

http://www.csi.ad.jp/ABOMB/index-j.html

This is an on-line museum recounting the history of the atomic bomb from a Japanese perspective.

Armies of the Second World War

http://www.sonic.net/~bstone/

This site contains a great variety of information about the war. It has unit histories, orders of battle, and links to other resources. It also includes a large bibliography of books about World War II and a feature that allows readers to post a list of books they are looking for.

Auschwitz: A Layman's Guide

http://www.almanac.bc.ca/faqs/auschwitz/index.html

Auschwitz: A Layman's Guide provides a broadly informative history of this notorious concentration camp.

Color Photographs from the Farm Security Administration and the Office of War Information

http://lcweb2.loc.gov/fsowhome.html

Photographs of rural and small-town America during the late 1930s and scenes of the defense and war mobilization efforts from 1939 to 1944.

Combat!

http://www.alegria.com/combat.html

Combat! discusses the classic World War II theme show that ran for five years in the 1960s. It contains a show overview, episode guides, and schedules of when and where you can watch the show in reruns.

Cybrary of the Holocaust

http://remember.org/

The Cybrary is an excellent resource for students and teachers of the Holocaust. It includes text-based learning materials, images, witness testimonials, and bibliographies.

Dad's War

http://members.aol.com/dadswar/index.html

This project intends to create a database of individual accounts of wartime experiences. It also allows the posting of queries about the war and contains information about World War II alumni associations.

Fall of Singapore

http://www.ncb.gov.sg/nhb/dec8/war.html

This Web site presents an account of the fall of Singapore to the Japanese Army on December 8, 1941. There is a narrative history, timeline, glossary, photographs, and a sound archive with radio broadcasts and excerpts of wartime speeches.

Fight Against Hate

gopher://gopher.jer1.co.il/11/fight

This site includes more than 6,000 documents on the Holocaust. Topics range from neo-Nazi skinheads and denials of the Holocaust to recommendations for teachers.

Fighters on the Farm Front

http://159.121.28.251/osuhomepage.html

Fighters on the Farm Front is an exhibit highlighting Oregon's Emergency Farm Labor Service during World War II. Text and photos cover POWs, women, migrant workers, and youth laborers.

George Rarey's Cartoon Journal of the 379th Fighter Squadron

http://www.nbn.com/home/rareybird/index.html

This on-line cartoon journal includes scanned images and text from the diaries and letters of George Rarey, an American fighter pilot during World War II.

Hiroshima and Nagasaki Exhibition

http://www.oneworld.org/gallery/hiroshima/hiroshima_top.html

The Hiroshima and Nagasaki Exhibition contains a collection of images provided by the World Conference Against Atom and Hydrogen Bombs. This is a graphic and moving multimedia site.

Holocaus

http://h-net2.msu.edu/~holoweb

This is the Web site of the Holocaus discussion list. Affiliated with H-Net, this group focuses on the history of the Holocaust. Their Web pages contain information about the discussion list and allow one to subscribe. They also include calls for papers, conference announcements, bibliographies, book reviews, articles, and links to related sites.

Holocaust: An Historical Summary

http://www.ushmm.org/education/history.html

This site presents a short summary of the Holocaust.

Holocaust Pictures Exhibition

http://modb.oce.ulg.ac.be/schmitz/holocaust.html

The Holocaust Pictures Exhibition includes thirty-seven images of the Holocaust at present, with more being added. A short description is given of each picture along with the photo's provenance. The descriptions are in English and French.

Holocaust Sites

http://www.almanac.bc.ca/other-sites/

This site is a gateway to many Holocaust-related Web pages. The list is broken down into four sub-categories: "Information About the Holocaust," "Rebuttals of Holocaust Denial," "Denial- or Racism-related," and the "Promotion of Holocaust-Denial."

Homefront Pictures 1938–1944

http://rs6.loc.gov/fsowhome.html

Over 1,600 color photographs from the Farm Security Administration and the Office of War Information are on-line at this Library of Congress site. The collection is searchable by key word and other methods, and each image is accompanied by background data. The site lists photographers, assignments, and how to order transparencies and photos.

I*EARN Holocaust/Genocide Project Web Site

http://www.peg.apc.org/~iearn/hgpproject.html

The I*EARN Project site offers bibliographies, syllabi, an electronic conference, and related links on the Holocaust and genocide.

Japanese War Crimes

http://www.cs.umn.edu/~dyue/wiihist/

This site chronicles the Japanese war crimes that occurred in China, particularly the rape of Nanking. Some parts are only in Chinese.

Keeping the Memory Alive

http://www.webbuild.com/~jbdavis/ww2.html

Keeping the Memory Alive contains a variety of images and posters about World War II. Maps of battlefronts, war reports, and a large number of links to related sites are also presented.

L'Chaim: A Holocaust Web Project

http://www.charm.net/~rbennett/l'chaim.html

Created by Robert Bennett, L'Chaim serves as a clearinghouse for Holocaust information. It contains an excellent virtual tour of the Dachau prison camp with photos and descriptions, survivors' tales, and a list of links to related sites. Note this site contains graphic and moving content.

Manhattan Project

http://www.needham.mec.edu/NPS_Web_docs/High_School/cur/mp/index.html

The Manhattan Project Web pages discuss the race to build the first atomic bomb. The site includes many color pictures of atomic bomb tests and the major scientists involved. It also has an excellent list of links to related sites.

Map Archive

http://192.253.114.31/D-Day/Maps_room/Map_room_contents.html

This on-line archive offers a great variety of maps for major battles of the European theater.

Mulvaney on Bomb Disposal

http://www.best.com/~thvv/mulvaney.html

This Web page contains a series of black-and-white, generally small, cartoons from the bomb disposal school's publications. It also includes a thirty-eight-page book issued during World War II for those in the bomb disposal division and cartoons done by Sergeant Robert Vittur.

Nanjing Massacre, 1937–1938

http://www.arts.cuhk.hk/NanjingMassacre/NM.html

This is a well-rounded site that gives testimonials about the massacre, as well as photographs, articles, timelines, and bibliographies. It also has a section that quotes the statements that Japanese officials made about the massacre.

The Nizkor Project

http://nizkor.almanac.bc.ca/

The Nizkor Project Web site is the home page of an international multimedia project, spearheaded by Canada-based archivist Ken McVay, which aims to counter those who deny the Holocaust. It is a well-documented and rich source containing more than four thousand documents.

Oral History Archives of World War II

http://history.rutgers.edu/orlhom.htm

The Oral History Archives aim to record the stories of those who fought in World War II.

Poster Art from World War II

http://www.nara.gov/exhall/wwii/powers/powers.html

This site contains several full-color posters from World War II.

Propaganda Posters

http://www.openstore.com/posters/

This Web page has twenty-two on-line posters from World War II. They are from a variety of organizations, including Navy Recruiting, the United States Civil Service Commission, and the Office of War Information.

Rescue of Bulgarian Jews During World War II

http://ASUdesign.eas.asu.edu/places/Bulgaria/Jewish/

Not a single Bulgarian Jew was deported to the Nazi death camps during World War II. Why was Bulgaria an exception? This site is an archive of articles and letters that document the experience of Jews in Bulgaria and attempt to answer this question.

Responses to the Holocaust

http://jefferson.village.virginia.edu/holocaust/response.html

The goal of Responses to the Holocaust is to provide a comprehensive source book on the Holocaust for students and teachers in the humanities. The site contains many primary documents that can be searched by text, author, or subject.

Salzburg 1945–1955: Liberators and Occupiers

http://www.image.co.at/image/salzburg

This site contains hypertext documents describing the postwar years in Salzburg. The supporting materials include maps, photos, military orders, and interviews with soldiers and civilians.

To Save a Life: Stories of Jewish Rescue

http://www.humboldt.edu/~rescuers/

To Save a Life is a previously unpublished work by Ellen Land-Weber that tells the stories of nine Jews who were rescued from the Holocaust and of the six people who helped to save them.

Select World War II Audiovisual Records from the National Archives

http://gopher.nara.gov:70/Oh/inform/dc/audvis/still/ww2photo.html

This National Archives on-line exhibit contains photographs that document both the homefront and military operations during World War II. The themes addressed include training, combat, support services, war production, and rest and relaxation.

The Simon Wiesenthal Center

http://www.wiesenthal.com

The Simon Wiesenthal Center in Los Angeles is dedicated to chronicling the history of human rights and the Holocaust. The Center's on-line site contains exhibits, glossaries, articles, information on the Center's activities, and more.

The U-Boat War, 1939–1945

http://rvik.ismennt.is/~gummihe/Uboats/u-boats.htm

This site presents photographs and biographical information about the men who commanded U-boats during World War II, complete with a listing of the number of ships they sank and the decorations they received. It also has information about U-boat types and builders and a list of the fates of various U-boats and their crews.

Warsaw Uprising

http://www.princeton.edu/~mkporwit/uprising/top.html

This Web page offers a multimedia history of the 1944 Warsaw Uprising, accompanied by maps and photos.

Wolf Lewkowicz Collection

http://web.mit.edu/maz/wolf/

The Wolf Lewkowicz Collection contains 178 letters in English from a man in Poland to another in the United States, written between 1922 and 1939. Wolf Lewkowicz was later sent to Treblinka where he died. Yiddish versions of the letters are also on-line, along with sound recordings. A list of names and a chronology of the letters is included to help researchers.

Women at War

http://wwwsun.redstone.army.mil/history/women.html

Women at War provides a detailed account of the women who worked at the Redstone Chemical Munitions Plant in Huntsville, Alabama, during World War II.

Women Come to the Front: Journalists, Photographers, and Broadcasters During World War II

http://lcweb.loc.gov/exhibits/wcf/wcf0001.html

Women Come to the Front spotlights eight women who covered World War II as journalists, photographers, and broadcasters. The exhibit is drawn primarily from a collection of the women's private papers and photographs which are part of the Library of Congress's holdings.

World War II

http://192.253.114.31/D-Day/GVPT_stuff/new.html

This site includes a variety of e-texts assembled by students and teachers at Patch High School in Germany. It has headlines from *Stars and Stripes,* pictures, documents, and movies.

World War II Archive

http://www.msstate.edu/Archives/History/USA/WWII/ww2.html

This is the World War II archive of Mississippi State University. It includes a good deal of information on Pearl Harbor and a number of documents, such as the Atlantic Charter and the Casablanca Conference proceedings.

World War II on the Internet

http://www.lib.muohio.edu/~skimmel/wwii/

World War II on the Internet contains some interesting facts and images from the Second World War. It also provides general links to World War II sites.

World War II Page

http://www.grolier.com/wwii/wwii_mainpage.html

The World War II page includes bibliographies, articles, photographs, air combat film clips, and a World War II quiz.

World War II Resources

gopher://ULKYVM.LOUISVILLE.EDU/11/library/govtpubs/subinfo/ /szsub/worwar

This is a gopher site from the University of Louisville containing links to a wide variety of documents. They include Chamberlain's "Peace in Our Time" speech, surrender documents, and Allied code names for Japanese aircraft.

World War II Veterans' Web Site

http://ww2.vet.org/

The World War II Veterans' Web site offers visitors the opportunity to post and view messages and memorabilia, contact lost friends, talk with other veterans, and find other World War II–related Web pages.

WWII Propaganda Posters

http://www.openstore.com/posters

This site contains several full-color World War II propaganda posters.

Yad Vashem

http://yvs.shani.net/

Yad Vashem is the Holocaust memorial established in Jerusalem in 1953. At present, the site contains on-line exhibits and information about the center.

THE KOREAN WAR

Dawn's Korean War Airplane Nose Art Page

http://www.tezcat.com/~dawn/warplane/warplane.html

This site contains a series of pictures taken of B-29s during the Korean War. It features the pictures on the front of the planes (nose art).

An Eyewitness: A Korean Remembers

http://www.kimsoft.com/korea/eyewit.htm

This page houses the memories of a Korean civilian who witnessed the Japanese occupation of Korea, the Soviet occupation of Korea (1945–1948), and the Korean War and the aftermath.

Korean War Project

http://www.onramp.net/~hbarker/

The Korean War Project site has links to Vietnam and Korean War casualty lists, information about the history of the Korean War, data on Korean War veterans' groups, and maps.

VIETNAM

Gopher to United States Government Documents on the Vietnam War

gopher://wiretap.spies.com/11/Gov/US-History/Vietnam

This site includes a growing number of documents on the Vietnam War. At present, the list includes the Gulf of Tonkin resolution, the State Department White Paper on Vietnam (1965), and a speech by John Kerry to the Senate in support of the Vietnam Veterans Against the War.

Images of My War

http://www.ionet.net/~uheller/vnbktoc.html

Images of My War contains a series of short essays describing one man's experiences in Vietnam.

The Sixties Project and the Vietnam Generation

http://jefferson.village.virginia.edu/sixties

The Sixties Project offers links to bibliographies, discussion groups, syllabi, and other Web sites of interest.

Vietnam Casualty Search

http://sersoft.clever.net/vietnam/

The Vietnam Casualty Search enables visitors to search a database of the recently released files on Vietnam War casualties.

THE GULF WAR

The Gulf War

http://www.pbs.org/pages/frontline/gulf/index.html

Developed by PBS to accompany a 1996 television special, this site looks at the Gulf War from a variety of angles. There are case studies of soldiers, politicians, and civilians; dozens of images; sound files; film clips; maps; and more.

Gulf War Photo Gallery

http://users.aol.com/andyhosk/gulf-war.html

The Gulf War Photo Gallery contains a large variety of color photos taken during the war by Ronald A. Hoskinson and from the library of Norman Jarvis. It includes pictures of life in the desert, of the troops' efforts at recreation, and of a night artillery attack.

RELIGIOUS HISTORY

Arianism

http://www.csn.net/advent/cathen/01707c.htm

This site presents a history of this early Christian sect and gives links to a few related sites.

Augustine on the Internet

http://ccat.sas.upenn.edu:80/jod/augustine.html

Augustine on the Internet contains a wealth of texts, commentaries and images relating to St. Augustine.

Buddhist Texts

http://www.uth.tmc.edu/~snewton/zen/index.shtml

This site offers a collection of historical and modern Buddhist texts.

The DILS Project

gopher://gopher.epas.utoronto.ca/11/cch/disciplines/medieval_studies /keefer

The DILS Project houses a database of religious manuscripts written in Anglo-Saxon England prior to 1100.

Druidism FAQ

http://www.reed.edu/~kday/druid.html

This FAQ contains a wide variety of miscellaneous information about the Druids.

The Ecole Initiative

http://cedar.evansville.edu/~ecoleweb/

The Ecole Initiative is an impressive hypertext encyclopedia of early (pre-Reformation) church history. The site has an extensive archive of primary source material under the "Documents" subheading; there are also many images and links to related materials.

Gnosis Archive

http://www.webcom.com/~gnosis

The Gnosis Archive serves as a clearinghouse for information, articles, and images relating to Gnostic theology and history.

Guide to Early Church Documents

http://www.iclnet.org/pub/resources/christian-history.html

This site contains links to sites on the early church, including canonical documents, creeds, the writings of the apostolic fathers, and other historical texts relevant to church history.

H-Judaic

http://h-net2.msu.edu/~judaic

This is the H-Judaic discussion list, which is dedicated to exploring Jewish history. The site contains information about the discussion list and allows one to subscribe. It also includes calls for papers, conference announcements, bibliographies, book reviews, articles, and links to related sites.

The Historical Jesus

http://www.willamette.edu/~tbrouwer/

This site provides a large collection of links to sites discussing the historical Jesus.

Islamic Scriptures and Prophetic Traditions

http://wings.buffalo.edu/hh/student-life/sa/muslim/isl/texts.html

This site is an excellent starting point for exploring texts and resources on sacred Islamic texts and related writings. It includes various Koran translations, articles on comparative scriptures, and historical essays.

Islamic Studies

http://menic.utexas.edu/menic/subject/islamic.html

Islamic Studies provides an index of links to many Web sites dedicated to the topic.

Islamic Texts and Resources MetaPage

http://wings.buffalo.edu:80/student-life/sa/muslim/isl/isl.html

The Islamic Texts and Resources MetaPage offers articles on Islam, FAQs regarding the practices of Islam, and links to resources for Islamic art, architecture, and culture.

Judaism and Jewish Resources

http://shamash.nysernet.org/trb/judaism.html

This is a major clearinghouse for Jewish resources on the Internet.

Latin Vulgate Bible

ftp://ftp.std.com/WWW/obi/Religion/Vulgate/

This is an FTP site for downloading sections of the Vulgate Bible.

Latin Vulgate Searchable Bible

http://humanities.uchicago.edu/forms_unrest/VULGATE.form.html

This on-line Vulgate Bible can be searched by particular names, words, or combinations of words.

The Philotheou Monastery Project

http://abacus.bates.edu/~rallison/index.html

This site provides scholars with information about the Philotheou Monastery manuscripts. Although you will not be able to see the actual manuscripts, this site provides valuable insight into the cataloging and preservation of manuscripts, as well as access to articles about the history of the Philotheou Monastery.

Project Genesis

http://www.torah.org/

Project Genesis offers Jewish seekers across the Internet a wide range of classes on Jewish philosophy, liturgy, ethics, and law. The classes are free, and one can subscribe or unsubscribe at any time.

Project Wittenberg

http://www.iclnet.org/pub/resources/text/wittenberg/wittenberg-home
.html

The Project Wittenberg site is dedicated to cataloging a cross section
of classic and historic texts written by Lutherans. These works are
posted in their original languages, in English translation, and in other
languages as available.

Rome Reborn: The Vatican Library and Renaissance Culture

http://sunsite.unc.edu/expo/vatican.exhibit/Vatican.exhibit.html

ftp://ftp.loc.gov/pub/exhibit.images/vatican.exhibit/

Rome Reborn contains scanned images from Renaissance manuscripts
owned by the Vatican Library. The images depict themes ranging from
humanism and medicine to music, mathematics, and nature.

Scrolls from the Dead Sea

http://sunsite.unc.edu/expo/deadsea.scrolls.exhibit/intro.html

ftp://ftp.loc.gov/pub/exhibit.images/deadsea.scroll.exhibit/

This site contains scanned images of Dead Sea scroll fragments, artifacts
from the Qumran site, manuscripts from the Library of Congress collection, and more. All of the scroll fragments have English translations.

Selected Early Christian Documents

http://web.mit.edu:80/afs/athena.mit.edu/activity/c/csa/www/documents/
README/

This site presents documents dating from A.D. 96–150, including several letters of Ignatius, bishop of Syria, and other writings of early
church fathers.

The Russian Church and Native Alaskan Cultures

http://lcweb.loc.gov/exhibits/russian/sa.html

ftp://ftp.loc.gov/pub/exhibit.images/russian.church

This site offers an exhibit tracing the experiences of Russian Orthodox
priests and Native Alaskans between the years 1794 and 1915. It includes photographs, lithographs, maps, and manuscripts.

Traditional Zoroastrianism

http://www.zip.com.au/~porushh/tenets33.html

This site discusses the philosophy and history of Zoroastrianism, as well as the historical background of the ancient Aryans.

Vedic Culture

http://zeta.cs.adfa.oz.au/Spirit/Veda/Overview.html

Vedic Culture is a collection of articles, essays, and book chapters that explore various aspects of Hindu culture. Topics covered include Vedic civilization in antiquity, cosmology, and Vedic life as it is practiced today.

World Scripture: A Comparative Anthology of Sacred Texts

http://www.silcom/~origin/wscon.html

This site comprises 150 entries on philosophical concepts such as the ideal society, marriage, ignorance, and cosmic justice. For each entry there is an essay and several excerpts from the sacred texts of world religions. The site addresses Islam, Christianity, Judaism, Hinduism, Taoism, African religions, and others.

HISTORIC PRESERVATION AND CONSERVATION

Advisory Council on Historic Preservation: Federal Agency Programs and Links

http://www.achp.gov/federal.html

This site chronicles the ever-changing government regulations affecting historic preservation and conservation.

Conservation On-Line

http://palimpsest.stanford.edu/

Conservation On-Line has a wide variety of conservation tips. It has links to conservation and preservation associations, guides that explain the conservation process for various items, and a host of other related materials.

DELLERCON

http://home.aol.com/DELLERCON

DELLERCON is dedicated to furniture and decorative arts. The page has many suggestions for those wishing to do their own restoration work, and it includes links to exhibits, guides, organizations, and related sites.

Federal Tax Credits for Historic Houses

http://www.historichouse.com/ft/tax2.htm

This site lists the government tax regulations that pertain to historic homes.

Historic Preservation Home Page

http://www.cadd.nps.usace.army.mil/tcx_psb/histpres.htm

The Historic Preservation Home Page is an excellent beginning point for anyone interested in preservation. It includes information on every conceivable aspect of preservation and restoration or a link to it.

Historical Book Preservation Project

http://www.jer1.co.il/orgs/archival/bookb2.htm

The Historical Book Preservation Project has detailed information on the preservation process, related societies, exhibits, archives and libraries, and other relevant themes.

National Trust for Historic Preservation Web Site

http://www.nthp.org/

This Web page presents all sorts of information about the National Trust for Historic Preservation. It includes a statement of purpose, a list of the most endangered historical sites in the United States, details on the group's services, membership information, and an explanation of how the society works to advance preservation.

PRESED-X, Preservation Educators' Exchange

http://www.well.com/user/bronxbob/presed-x/presed-x.html

PRESED-X is a forum for teachers and professors of preservation. It includes an excellent collection of links to preservation-related education resources.

Preservation Resources

http://www.preservation.org/links.html

Preservation Resources is a large collection of links to preservation and conservation sites.

Preserve/Net

http://www.preservenet.cornell.edu/

Preserve/Net is an indexed guide to programs and sites dedicated to historic preservation.

Readings in Preservation

http://palimpsest.stanford.edu/byorg/solinet/presbib.htm

This site provides an introductory bibliography for newcomers to preservation.

Teaching with Historic Places Home Page

http://www.cr.nps.gov/nr/twhp/home.html

This site offers an innovative description of how teachers can use field trips to historic places to teach broad aspects of history. The site has many good suggestions for educators.

HISTORICAL REENACTMENT

Association for Living Historical Farms and Agricultural Museums

http://www.mystic.org/~alhfam/

This site includes membership information, a bibliography, annual meeting notes, and Web links.

English Civil War Society

http://www.jpbooks.com/ecws/

This site discusses the English Civil War Society's organization, membership, and activities. There is also a large collection of reviews, bibliographies, photographs, and sound files.

Living History Bibliography

http://www.mystic.org/~alhfam/alhfam.bib.html

This is an on-line bibliography dedicated to living history.

Reenactor Net

http://www.reenactor.net/

Reenactor Net contains an indexed catalog of links to reenactment societies, events, and organizations in Australia, Canada, Great Britain, and the United States.

Renaissance Faire Page

http://sundry.hsc.usc.edu/faire.html

This site provides a calendar of Renaissance fairs across North America. There are also links to fair home pages, guild and troupe sites, and individual reenactors' Web pages.

Society for Creative Anachronism

http://pacifier.com/~phil/index.html

The Society for Creative Anachronism is the largest medieval reenactment society in the United States. This site provides information about the group's activities and links to local chapters.

GENEALOGY

Cool Sites for Genealogists

http://www.cogensoc.org/cgs/cgs-cool.htm

Cool Sites for Genealogists lists interesting sites that genealogists should visit. The Web pages are sponsored by the Colorado Genealogical Society, and a new "unknown" site is added each month.

Everton's *Genealogical Helper:* On-Line Edition

http://www.everton.com/

This site hosts an on-line version of Everton's popular *Genealogical Helper,* which offers tips to those conducting genealogical research.

Genealogy

http://ftp.cac.psu.edu/~saw/genealogy-full.html

Everything you ever wanted to know about genealogy, but were afraid to ask. This site includes guides, maps, on-line information, and links to related sites. It also contains information on societies and events and details about discussion groups that treat genealogy.

Genealogy BBS List

http://www.genealogy.org/~gbbs/

This list is updated monthly and contains over one thousand bulletin boards. The BBS numbers are indexed by state and links are provided to related sites. The site is a service of the National Genealogical Society.

Genealogy Chat

http://www.irsociety.com/cgi-bin/webchat_doorway.cgi/Room=Genea logy

A discussion forum on genealogical topics.

Genealogy Dictionary

http://www.electriciti.com/~dotts/diction.html#DICT

A huge dictionary of the terms likely to be encountered while doing genealogical research.

The Genealogy Home Page

http://ftp.cac.psu.edu/~saw/genealogy.html

This Web page contains on-line genealogical information, information about genealogical software, a calendar of upcoming events, and links to related sites.

Genealogy Listservs, Newsgroups, and Special Home Pages

http://www.eskimo.com/~chance/

This is a large database of links to genealogy sites.

GenMatch

http://www.jpunix.com/~ckp/genmatch/genmatch.htm

GenMatch is a database that allows you to search a number of sites for references to your ancestor.

GenTutor

http://home.aol.com/GenTutor

GenTutor is a step-by-step guide to genealogical research. The site contains links to many sites that can help budding genealogists.

Historical Genealogy Department—
Fort Wayne, Indiana

http://www.acpl.lib.in.us/departments/genealogy.html

This site is sponsored by the second largest North American genealogical repository. It includes information on how to get started, resources for specific states and countries, and reports on specific topics.

Royal Genealogies

http://ftp.cac.psu.edu/~saw/royal/royalgen.html

This site provides genealogies for many of the royal houses of Europe.

STATE HISTORICAL SOCIETIES

The state historical societies listed below have Web pages. All of these sites contain information about the societies' activities, collections, and hours. These state historical societies also sponsor on-line exhibitions of the materials in their collections. The exhibits change often, however, so detailed descriptions are not given below. Anyone interested in local history will find these evolving sites invaluable.

California Historical Society

http://www.calhist.org

Hawaiian Historical Society Library

http://www.aloha.com/~mem/libmain.html

Illinois State Historical Society
http://alexia.lis.uiuc.edu/~sorensen/hist.html

Indiana Historical Society
http://www.spcc.com/ihsw/ihs.html

Kansas State Historical Society
http://history.cc.ukans.edu/heritage/kshs/kshs1.html

Michigan Historical Center
http://www.sos.state.mi.us/history/history.html

Minnesota Historical Society
http://www.umn.edu/nlhome/g075/mnshpo/index.html

Missouri Historical Society
http://www.vstl.com/mhs_home.html

New Hampshire Historical Society
http://newww.com/org/nhhs/library.html

Ohio Historical Society
http://winslo.ohio.gov/ohswww/ohshome.html

Oregon Historical Society—Oregon History Center
http://www.fpa.pdx.edu/depts/fpa/html/ohs.html

Pennsylvania Historical and Museum Commission
http://www.state.pa.us/PA_Exec/Historical_Museum/DAM/overview
.htm

South Carolina Historical Society
http://www.historic.com/schs/

State Historical Society of Wisconsin
http://www.wisc.edu/shs-archives/

Texas State Historical Association
http://www.dla.utexas.edu/texhist/

Washington State Historical Society

http://www.ci.tacoma.wa.us/cgi-bin/details.pl?gallery+30

HISTORICAL ORGANIZATIONS AND ASSOCIATIONS

The sites listed below all contain detailed information about their sponsoring organizations and many resources relating to their special emphases. Descriptions are provided only for those organizations whose aims may not be clear from their names.

American Academy of Arts and Sciences

http://www.amacad.org:80

American Academy of Research Historians of Medieval Spain

http://kuhttp.cc.ukans.edu/kansas/aarhms/mainpage.html

American Antiquarian Society

gopher://mark.mwa.org:70/0briefaccount.text

The American Antiquarian Society is one of the oldest scholarly associations in the United States. It sponsors a wide variety of historical and cultural research; its Web site lists its activities and details the results of the research efforts it supports.

American Association for State and Local History

http://www.Nashville.Net/~aaslh/

This site contains links to many state and local history organizations.

American Association of University Presses

http://aaup.pupress.princeton.edu:70/

American Cultural Resources Association

http://www.mindspring.com/~wheaton/ACRA.html

The American Historical Association

http://web.gmu.edu/chnm/aha/

This is the oldest and largest organization of historians in America.

American Jewish Historical Society

http://www.tiac.net/users/ajhs/

American Society of Papyrologists

http://scholar.cc.emory.edu/scripts/ASP/ASP-MENU.html

Architectural Heritage Society of Scotland

http://www.ahss.org.uk/

The Association of Asian Studies

http://bbanning.memorial.indiana.edu/~aas/

Association for Gravestone Studies

http://www.history.rochester.edu/ags/ags.html

The Association for History and Computing

http://grid.let.rug.nl/ahc/welcome.html

The Association for History and Computing is an international organization that aims to promote and develop teaching and research interest in the use of computers for all types of historical study at every level.

Association for Living Historical Farms and Agricultural Museums

http://www.mystic.org/~alhfam/

Center for History and New Media

http://web.gmu.edu/chnm/

Located at George Mason University, this group works to explore the promise of history in the electronic age.

Cherokee National Historical Society

http://www.powersource.com/powersource/heritage/default.html

Chicago Historical Society

http://www.chicagohs.org/

Cliometric Society

http://cs.muohio.edu/ehs_text.shtml

A national society dedicated to research in various fields of economic history.

Computer History Association of California

http://www.chac.org/chac/

Economic History Association

http://cs.muohio.edu/ehs_text.shtml

The Historical Society Page

http://www2.cybernex.net/~manty/

This page provides information about and links to many historical organizations and societies. It has a wealth of information that will interest scholars and history buffs alike.

History of Science Society

http://weber.u.washington.edu/~hssexec/index.html

International Council on Archives

http://www.archives.ca/ica/

International Society of Anglo-Saxonists

http://www.as.wvu.edu/english/isas/

International Students of History Association

http://hagar.arts.kuleuven.ac.be/org/isha/

Medieval Academy of America

http://www.georgetown.edu/MedievalAcademy/

Middle East Studies Association

http://www.cua.edu/www/mesabul/welcome.htm

National Association of Scholars

http://www.nas.org/nas.htm

National Coordinating Committee for the Promotion of History

http://h-net2.msu.edu/~ncc/

This committee is composed of members from more than fifty historical associations and is dedicated to the support of historical research and instruction. The site is a large clearinghouse for information.

National Council for the Social Studies

http://www.ncss.org/home/ncss

Organization of American Historians

http://www.indiana.edu/~oah

Scholarly Societies on the Web

http://www.lib.uwaterloo.ca/society/overview.html

A periodically updated list of historical associations that have Internet sites.

SHARP Web

http://www.indiana.edu/~sharp/

SHARP is the Society for the History of Authorship, Reading, and Publishing. Their Web site provides links to publishers' Web pages with historical materials, other projects, resources, and scholarly societies with an interest in the history of print culture.

Society for the History of Technology

http://hfm.umd.umich.edu/tc/SHOT/

The Voltaire Foundation

http://www.voltaire.ox.ac.uk/

An international society dedicated to fostering study and publication on the Enlightenment.

MAPS

Heritage Map Museum

http://www.carto.com/

This is a commercial site which sells fifteenth- through nineteenth-century original antique maps.

Historical Atlas of Europe

http://www.ma.org/maps/map.html

This historical atlas is indexed by era, and it covers the period from 3000 B.C. to the present. For each historical period, a variety of maps are presented and each map contains a brief historical sketch.

Historical Maps

http://www.ma.org/maps/map.html

This site has a good selection of full-color maps for historical periods from the Bronze Age to the present.

The Map Archive

http://192.253.114.31/D-Day/Maps_room/Map_room_contents.html

The Map Archive contains a great variety of maps for major battles in the European theater.

Map Projection Home Page

http://everest.hunter.cuny.edu/mp/

This site is dedicated to cartographic history.

Maps of Europe

http://www.stg.brown.edu/projects/hypertext/landow/victorian/victov.
html

The Maps of Europe site contains more than 230,000 current maps of continents, regions, and countries.

New York State Maps: Cartographic Images Created Prior to 1830

http://www.sunysb.edu/library/ldmaps.htm

This site has full-color maps of the New York area dating from 1556 to 1825.

Paris Maps

http://www.cc.columbia.edu/imaging/html/paris.html

gopher://gutentag.cc.columbia.edu:70/11/fun/pictures/art-history

Paris Maps includes one hundred full-color maps of eighteenth- and nineteenth-century Paris.

Perry-Castaneda Library Map Collection

http://www.lib.utexas.edu/Libs/PCL/Map_collection/Map_collection.
html

The Perry-Castaneda Library map collection contains a wide selection of historical and contemporary maps.

Perseus Atlas Project

http://perseus.holycross.edu/PAP/Atlas_project.html

The Perseus Atlas Project is developing an extensive general-purpose geographic information system for the study of classical Greece. At present this database has been built entirely from printed sources. The site also provides access to an electronic version of Stephanus of Byzantium's *Ethnica*—a Greek lexicon of more than 3,500 geographic and ethnographic proper names.

Rare Map Collection

http://scarlett.libs.uga.edu/darchive/hargrett/maps/maps.html

This Web site contains more than 150 rare maps from 1600 to 1870.

ELECTRONIC TEXTS

The term "electronic texts" is broad and often confusing. For the purposes of this book, the following types of items will be considered e-texts:

Books. This refers to actual electronic versions of books. Due to copyright restrictions, most of these books are more than seventy-five years old and are in the public domain. There are attempts by organizations such as Project Gutenberg to scan the full text of certain books into the Internet. Such books can be downloaded and printed out for easier reading. Once you have an electronic copy of a text, you can also manipulate the text with a variety of database, spreadsheet, word processor, and search programs.

Historic Documents. This refers to the full text of historic documents such as the *Federalist Papers,* United Nations treaties, or the transcript of Roosevelt's Declaration of War on Japan. There are some more obscure documents being made available as well, such as historic treaties between the United States and Native Americans, or documents being declassified from the Soviet Union.

Scanned Documents. This refers to photographic reproductions of items that are scanned into the Internet, such as medieval Irish manuscripts or letters from a Civil War soldier.

Ephemera. This includes a variety of interesting, mostly unpublished items from private collections. Examples include unpublished diaries from the Civil War, a collection of French Revolution pamphlets, and the lyrics of folk songs that have never found their way into a published format. This is one of the great uses of the Internet, since items that would otherwise not be available can now be disseminated to the public.

GENERAL

ALEX: A Catalog of Electronic Texts on the Internet

http://dewey.lib.ncsu.edu/stacks/alex-index.html

gopher://gopher.lib.ncsu.edu:70/11/library/stacks/Alex

Alex contains a searchable catalog of nearly two thousand texts, including classic literary works, commentaries, government documents, and more.

The Electronic Text Center

http://etext.lib.virginia.edu/center.html

This site provides access to a tremendous amount of electronic resources, including the *Oxford English Dictionary,* the complete works of Shakespeare, several versions of the Bible, and much more. It supports software packages that allow scholars to build indices, concordances, and word lists or conduct statistical and textual analysis. The only down side is that it is only available to people associated with the University of Virginia. The general public can visit their home page, though, and this may be worthwhile, in that it can teach you about the possibilities for electronic manipulation of text.

The English Server at Carnegie Mellon

http://english-www.hss.cmu.edu/history.html

This site contains a good collection of articles on various aspects of history. It is part of a larger collection that also covers literature, art, philosophy, politics, and more.

Historical Documents

gopher://ucsbuxa.ucsb.edu:3001/11/.stacks/.historical

This site offers documents relating to American history. It contains the full texts of famous treaties, charters, and speeches. Examples include the Mayflower Compact, the Monroe Doctrine, Washington's Farewell Address, and Martin Luther King's "I Have a Dream" speech.

Historical Text Archive

gopher://dewey.lib.ncsu.edu/11/library/disciplines/history/archives

http://www.msstate.edu/Archives/History/

Maintained at Mississippi State University, the Historical Text Archive provides access to the full text of selected historical documents from around the world (constitutions, charters, and speeches). It is the oldest historical FTP site in the United States, and it has extensive holdings to match its age.

On-Line Book Page

http://www.cs.cmu.edu/Web/books.html

The On-Line Book Page provides access to more than nine hundred electronic books.

Project Gutenberg

http://www.vuw.ac.nz/non-local/gutenberg/home.html

Project Gutenberg coordinates a volunteer effort for the public release of electronic editions of classical literature and reference material.

Wiretap E-Text Releases

gopher://wiretap.spies.com:70/11/Books

Wiretap E-Text Releases is a collection of literature that is in the public domain. It includes fiction, nonfiction, and philosophical works.

ANCIENT AND MEDIEVAL

Ancient Texts

gopher://ccat.sas.upenn.edu:3333/11/Classical

Ancient Texts contains e-texts from classical authors such as Aesop, Homer, and Sophocles.

Anglo-Saxon Texts

ftp://ftp.std.com/WWW/obi/Anglo-Saxon

This is an FTP site for downloading or viewing historical Anglo-Saxon texts.

CURIA: Irish Manuscripts Project

http://curia.ucc.ie/curia/menu.html

The mission of the CURIA project is to provide an interactive on-line searchable database archive of literary and historical materials in the various languages of early, medieval, and modern Ireland.

Labyrinth Library

http://www.georgetown.edu/labyrinth/library/library.html

The Labyrinth Library contains full-text versions of medieval documents and literature. The works presently on-line include religious writings, poetry, legal documents, and some reference works. Texts appear in the following languages: Latin, Old English, Middle English, French, and Italian.

Mayan Epigraphic Database Project

http://jefferson.village.virginia.edu/med/home.html

The Mayan Epigraphic Database Project is compiling a collection of primary and secondary sources that show the evolution of Mayan script. The site includes a glyph catalog.

Medieval Books in Electronic Format

http://www.cs.cmu.edu/afs/andrew.cmu.edu/org/Medieval/www/src/medieval/periodbook.html

This site provides full-text access to a number of medieval plays, letters, and poems.

The Middle English Collection at the University of Virginia

http://etext.virginia.edu/me.browse.html

This site presents full-text versions of many Middle English plays, poems, and philosophical writings.

The Perseus Project

http://medusa.perseus.tufts.edu/Texts.html

The Perseus Project contains a huge searchable database of ancient Greek texts in the original Greek as well as English translations. The site includes software that permits textual analysis, word frequency counts, and morphological analysis.

Project Runeberg

http://www.lysator.liu.se/runeberg

gopher://gopher.lysator.liu.se/

Project Runeberg is an initiative to collect and create electronic editions of classic Nordic literature and art.

RELIGIOUS HISTORY

Buddhist Texts

http://www.uth.tmc.edu/~snewton/zen/index.shtml

This site contains a collection of historical and modern Buddhist texts.

The Ecole Initiative

http://cedar.evansville.edu/~ecoleweb/

The Ecole Initiative is a hypertext encyclopedia of (pre-Reformation) church history. This site has an extensive archive of primary source material under the "Documents" subheading.

Guide to Early Church Documents

http://www.iclnet.org/pub/resources/christian-history.html

This site contains links to materials on the early church, including canonical documents, creeds, the writings of the apostolic fathers, and other historical texts relevant to church history.

Islamic Scriptures and Prophetic Traditions

http://wings.buffalo.edu/hh/student-life/sa/muslim/isl/texts.html

This site is an excellent starting point for exploring texts and resources on sacred Islamic texts and related writings. It includes various Koran translations, articles on comparative scriptures, and historical essays.

Latin Vulgate Bible

ftp://ftp.std.com/WWW/obi/Religion/Vulgate/

This is an FTP site for downloading sections of the Vulgate Bible.

Latin Vulgate Searchable Bible

http://humanities.uchicago.edu/forms_unrest/VULGATE.form.html

This on-line version of the Vulgate Bible can be searched by particular names, words, or combinations of words.

Project Wittenberg

http://www.iclnet.org/pub/resources/text/wittenberg/wittenberg-home.html

The Project Wittenberg site is dedicated to cataloging a cross section of classic and historic texts written by Lutherans. These works are posted in their original languages, in English translation, and in other languages as available.

Selected Early Christian Documents

http://web.mit.edu:80/afs/athena.mit.edu/activity/c/csa/www/documents/README/

This site presents documents dating from A.D. 96–150, including several letters of Ignatius, bishop of Syria, and other writings of early church fathers.

Traditional Zoroastrianism

http://www.zip.com.au/~porushh/tenets33.html

This site discusses the philosophy and history of Zoroastrianism, as well as the historical background of the ancient Aryans.

Vedic Culture

http://zeta.cs.adfa.oz.au/Spirit/Veda/Overview.html

Vedic Culture is a collection of articles, essays, and book chapters that explore various aspects of Hindu culture. Topics covered include Vedic civilization in antiquity, cosmology, and Vedic life as it is practiced today.

World Scripture—A Comparative Anthology of Sacred Texts

http://www.silcom.com/~origin/wscon.html

This site comprises 150 entries on philosophical concepts such as the ideal society, marriage, ignorance, and cosmic justice. For each entry there is an essay and several excerpts from the sacred texts of world religions. The site addresses Islam, Christianity, Judaism, Hinduism, Taoism, African religions, and others.

AMERICAN HISTORY

African-American Historical Documents

gopher://UMSLVMA.UMSL.EDU/11/LIBRARY/SUBJECTS/BLACK STU/BLACKCOL

This site has a wide variety of texts relating to African-American history.

American and British History Electronic Archives, Texts, and Journals

http://info.rutgers.edu/rulib/artshum/amhist.html

This site serves as a clearinghouse for full-text historical documents. Under the subheading "Electronic Archives, Texts and Journals," you will find links to various sites that contain a wide range of historical documents.

American Civil War—Documents and Books

http://www.access.digex.net/~bdboyle/docs.html

This site presents a number of contemporary letters, diaries, and other documents relating to the Civil War.

American Memory

http://rs6.loc.gov/amhome.html

American Memory is a tremendous collection of historical texts and images from the National Digital Library Project of the Library of Congress. The site includes an impressive array of primary and archival documents relating to United States history. There are hundreds of photographs and documents from the National Archives and Library of Congress already on-line, and the number is being increased steadily. The site also includes sound files and early American movies from 1897 to 1916. All of the resources in the collection can be searched in a variety of ways.

Benjamin Franklin's Collected Works

gopher://gopher.vt.edu:10010/11/85

This site contains full-text versions of many of Benjamin Franklin's works.

A Chronology of United States Historical Documents

http://www.law.uoknor.edu/ushist.html#ind

Compiled by the Law Center of the University of Oklahoma, this site presents a documentary history of the United States from the Magna Carta to Bill Clinton's 1996 State of the Union Address. The documents in this collection make an excellent teaching resource.

Civil War Documents and Books

http://www.access.digex.net/~bdboyle/docs.html

This site offers access to the full texts of Civil War books, historical documents, collections of letters, and speeches.

Confederate States of America Document Collection

http://www.snider.net/home/color/csadoc.htm

This on-line Civil War collection contains many documents from the Confederate States of America.

Decisions of the United States Supreme Court

http://www.law.cornell.edu/supct/supct.table.html

This site includes a searchable database of Supreme Court decisions. Only decisions dating back to 1990 are presently on-line, but more are being added regularly.

Diaries from Pennsylvania and Virginia

http://jefferson.village.virginia.edu/vshadow/diary.html

This Web page contains selections from six diaries, dating mostly from the Civil War.

The Federalist Papers

http://www.law.uoknor.edu/hist/federalist.html

This site contains selections from *The Federalist Papers.*

How the Other Half Lives

http://www.cis.yale.edu/amstud/inforev/riis/title.html

How the Other Half Lives is a hypertext edition of Jacob Riis' classic 1890 book, which exposed the conditions of life in New York City tenements. The site includes many of the photographs that moved readers of the original book.

Inaugural Addresses of American Presidents

gopher://gopher.cc.columbia.edu:71/11/miscellaneous/cubooks/inaug

This site contains the full-text inaugural speeches of every United States president who participated in an inaugural ceremony. There have been five presidents who were never inaugurated and merely took the oath of office (John Tyler, Millard Fillmore, Andrew Johnson, Chester A. Arthur, and Gerald R. Ford).

Letters Home from an Iowa Soldier in the Civil War

http://www.ucsc.edu/civil-war-letters/home.html

This site contains the letters Private Newton Robert Smith wrote to his sweetheart and his parents during the Civil War.

Life History Manuscripts from the Folklore Project, WPA Federal Writers' Project, 1936–1940

http://lcweb2.loc.gov/wpaintro/wpahome.html

This site includes interviews from the Federal Writers' Folklore Project, which detail the histories of Americans from many walks of life. The broad topics covered include "African-Americans," "Agriculture," "Immigration," "Labor," "Recreation," and "Women."

NativeWeb

http://web.maxwell.syr.edu/nativeweb/

NativeWeb provides full-text access to Native American poetry, stories, prayers, and famous documents.

Originals of Early American Documents

http://www.law.emory.edu/FEDERAL/conpict.html#const

This site contains scanned images of early American documents, including the Constitution, Bill of Rights, and Declaration of Independence.

The Papers of George Washington

http://www.virginia.edu/~gwpapers

This site is an archive of Washingtonian papers. Many papers are available on-line and information is given on the efforts to publish a comprehensive eighty-five-volume collection of all his writings.

State Department Publications and Reports

http://www.state.gov/index.html

This site contains many documents from the State Department. The site includes the Background Note Series, which provides practical information about the climate, culture, and living conditions of every country in the world; country reports on economic conditions and human rights; and reports on global terrorism.

United States Historical Documents

gopher://wiretap.spies.com/11/Gov/US-History

This site presents gopher links to a great number of historical documents. Among the documents presented are some of *The Federalist Papers,* the 1775 Declaration of Arms, the Monroe Doctrine, materials on the 1960 U–2 downing, and the two surrender declarations that ended World War II.

United States House of Representatives Internet Law Library

http://law.house.gov/1.htm

This site includes the latest budget, the *Code of Federal Regulations,* excerpts from the *Congressional Record,* texts of treaties, and international law documents.

United States Laws Relating to Indian Nations and Tribes

http://law.house.gov/31.htm

This site includes on-line versions of many historical and contemporary texts and laws affecting Native Americans.

INTERNATIONAL

Documents on Mexican Politics

http://daisy.uwaterloo.ca/~alopez-o/polind.html

This is a large file of articles relating to current Mexican politics and economics. Most of the articles are of current interest, rather than on historical topics. There are also some Mexican government documents and official documents from Mexican political parties.

Documents Room

http://kuhttp.cc.ukans.edu/carrie/docs_main.html

The Documents Room contains letters, speeches, constitutions, memoirs, and the charters and treaties of the United States, the United Nations, and the Catholic Church.

EuroDocs

http://library.byu.edu/~rdh/eurodocs/

This is Brigham Young University's collection of on-line primary historical documents from Western Europe, including selected transcriptions, facsimiles, and translations. The entries cover political, economic, social, and cultural history.

Fourth World Documentation Project

http://www.halcyon.com/FWDP/fwdp.html

gopher://locust.cic.net/11/Politics/Fourth.World

This site presents "fourth world documents and resources." The project defines the fourth world as "nations forcefully incorporated into states which maintain a distinct political culture but are internationally unrecognized."

French Revolutionary Pamphlets

http://humanities.uchicago.edu/homes/mark/fr_rev.html

This Web site presents scanned images from pamphlets produced during the French Revolution. A small collection at present, but planning to expand.

German Surrender Documents

http://library.byu.edu/~rdh/eurodocs/germ/germsurr.html

This site contains an extensive collection of documents relating to Germany's terms of surrender at the end of World War II.

International Affairs Primary Documents

http://www.pitt.edu/~ian/resource/primary.htm

The International Affairs Primary Documents page contains documents relating to international law, international security, world trade, world finance, the armed forces, and the Arab-Israeli conflict.

Japanese Surrender Documents, 1945

gopher://wiretap.spies.com:70/00/Gov/US-History/japan.sur

This is a collection of documents relating to Japanese terms of surrender in 1945.

Library of Historical Documents

telnet://freenet.victoria.bc.ca

The Library of Historical Documents includes a wide variety of documents, many relating to Canada.

The Monde Diplomatique

http://www.ina.fr/CP/MondeDiplo/mondediplo.fr.html

The Monde Diplomatique is a French text archive for materials on economic, political, and cultural events worldwide.

Revelations from the Russian Archives

http://sunsite.unc.edu/expo/soviet.exhibit/soviet.archive.html

Revelations from the Russian Archives contains documents from the former Soviet Union. The site includes both original-language versions and English translations for most documents. The exhibit has two sections, the first focusing on domestic Soviet issues, the second dealing with Soviet-American relations.

Soviet Archives

gopher://gopher.tamu.edu:70/11/.dir/soviet.archives.dir

This Web site contains selected documents recently declassified from the Soviet Archives. The documents date from 1917 through the failed coup attempt in 1991 and include papers from the working files of the Central Committee, the Presidential Archive, and the KGB.

Soviet Studies Research Center

gopher://gopher.nato.int/11/secdef/csrc

The Soviet Studies Research Center home page provides an extensive listing of full-text documents relating to Russian military, political, and social issues. Examples of the themes covered by the documents now on-line include the crisis in Chechnya, military justice, Russian relations with the Middle East, and the problems of economic reforms. All reports are written by analysts affiliated with the Conflict Studies Research Center—a British think tank.

Stories of the Famine

http://www.emory.edu/FAMINE/

Stories of the Famine includes full-text articles from the *Illustrated London News* covering the Irish potato famine. The site also includes links to fifty-six accompanying engravings.

World History Archives

http://library.ccsu.ctstateu.edu/~history/world_history/archives/

The World History Archives are a repository for documents that encourage an understanding of world history and the struggle for social progress. There is a lot of information here relating to the Third World, global economic forces, women's liberation, socialism, and communism.

MISCELLANEOUS

The Camelot Project

http://rodent.lib.rochester.edu/camelot/cphome.htm

This site was created by the University of Rochester Robbins Library. The site is a major resource for both scholars and history buffs. It contains the full texts of many Arthurian tales, an impressive collection of images, bibliographies, a searchable character index, and links to related sites.

Encyclopedia Mystica

http://www.pantheon.org/myth

This site contains an encyclopedia that treats magic, myths, legends, and folklore from all over the world and from all times.

Historical Philosophy

gopher://catfish.valdosta.peachnet.edu:70/11/ccr/subjv/phi/texts

This site provides access to the writings of famous philosophers, as well as essays on their works and other philosophical problems.

Hume Archives

http://unix1.utm.edu/departments/phil/hume.html

In addition to the texts of the Scottish philosopher David Hume, this site makes available contemporary and modern reviews and commentaries on Hume's work.

Project Aldus

http://www.jhu.edu/~english/aldus/aldus.main.html

Project Aldus is an electronic archive for primary and secondary materials relating to the English Renaissance and the early modern period.

Royal Genealogical Data

http://www.dcs.hull.ac.uk/public/genealogy/royal/catalog.html

This is a searchable database on European royalty from ancient times to the present.

HISTORICAL LITERATURE

The Art of War by Sun-Tzu

http://www.chinapage.com/sunzi-e.html

The complete text of this sixth-century-B.C. classic is provided in the original Chinese, along with an English translation.

ARTFL: American and French Research on the Treasury of the French Language

http://humanities.uchicago.edu/ARTFL/ARTFL.html

ARTFL contains electronic versions of nearly two thousand texts, which range from classic works of French literature to nonfiction prose to technical writing. The subjects covered include literary criticism, biology, history, economics, and philosophy. The database is presently available only to members of universities who are associated with the ARTFL project, but those with access can perform an impressive variety of intratextual and comparative textual searches.

Complete Works of William Shakespeare

http://the-tech.mit.edu/Shakespeare/works.html

This site contains the complete works of Shakespeare in downloadable and searchable format.

Dante Project

http://www.ilt.columbia.edu/projects/dante/index.html

The Dante Project intends to provide multimedia versions of Dante's works that can serve as research and teaching tools. The site currently contains several original versions and translations of *The Divine Comedy* which are illustrated and accompanied by a hypertext-linked commentary.

Electronic Beowolf Project

http://portico.bl.uk/access/beowulf/electronic-beowulf.html

The Electronic Beowolf Project has assembled a huge database of digital images of the Beowulf manuscript and related manuscripts and printed texts. The archive includes fiber-optic readings of hidden letters and ultraviolet readings of erased text in the early eleventh-century manuscript, full electronic facsimiles of the indispensable eighteenth-century transcripts of the manuscript, and selections from important nineteenth-century collections, editions, and translations.

Great Books of Western Civilization

http://www.ilinks.net/~lnoles/grtbks.html

This site is arranged around eight courses that Mercer University teaches covering the history of great books. Each section has a course description and the full texts of the assigned books.

Marx and Engels Full-Text Library

gopher://csf.colorado.edu/11/psn/Marx

The Marx and Engels Full-Text Library contains on-line versions of many of the writings, letters, and speeches of Marx and Engels.

Nineteenth-Century German Stories

http://www.fln.vcu.edu/menu.html

Beautifully illustrated with original manuscript drawings and etchings, this is a collection of nineteenth-century German stories, many of them from the Brothers Grimm. In the original German with English translations.

Piers Plowman Project

http://jefferson.village.virginia.edu/piers/archive.goals.html

The Piers Plowman Project is a multi-level, hyper-textually-linked electronic archive of the textual tradition of all three versions of the fourteenth-century allegorical story *Piers Plowman.*

Recovered Notebooks from the Walt Whitman Collection

http://lcweb2.loc.gov/ammem/wwhome.html

This site offers access to four Walt Whitman notebooks from the Library of Congress.

Voice of the Shuttle

http://humanitas.ucsb.edu/shuttle/english.html

Voice of the Shuttle is an outstanding site for research on English literature from all periods. It is arranged by chronological time period, with each section listing prominent authors, course syllabi, electronic journals, criticism, conference information, and calls for papers.

Writing Black USA

http://www.keele.ac.uk/depts/as/Literature/amlit.black.html

Writing Black USA contains full-text essays, books, and poems documenting the African-American experience in the United States from the colonial times to the present.

RESOURCES FOR TEACHERS AND PROFESSORS OF HISTORY

AcademicNet

http://www.academic.com/

AcademicNet provides a forum for educators who are interested in technology and higher education. You must register the first time you visit the site and then wait for approval before use. Events held all over the country are listed here.

American Studies Page

http://www.ilt.columbia.edu/k12/livetext/amstud.html

The American Studies Page contains lesson plans, student projects, on-line activities, and indices to other Internet resources for the study of American history and culture.

Archeological Fieldwork Server

http://durendal.cit.cornell.edu/testpit.html

The Archeological Fieldwork Server publicizes opportunities for archeological fieldwork around the world. The database includes listings for paid work, volunteer work, and field schools.

AskERIC Virtual Library

http://ericir.syr.edu

telnet://ericir.syr.edu

The AskERIC Virtual Library archives hundreds of lesson plans in a variety of disciplines, informational guides on topics of concern to K–12 educators, links to the searchable databases of ERIC Digests (which are brief reports on educational issues), information on using the Internet in the classroom, and links to other Internet sites.

Center for International Higher Education

http://www.bc.edu/bc_org/avp/soe/cihe/Center.html

This site contains information about the Center for International Higher Education and its activities. There are valuable discussions of teaching and links to educational sites.

Chronicle of Higher Education: ACADEME THIS WEEK

http://chronicle.merit.edu/.index.html#events

This on-line publication presents a weekly chronicle of important and entertaining events occurring in the academy.

Computing and History

gopher://gopher.epas.utoronto.ca:70/11/cch/hum_comp/courses/essays/davis_denley_spaeth_trainor

Computing and History presents a series of essays about various ways computers can be used by historians. The essays covers items such as "Oral History and Computing," "Computing and the Middle Ages," and "Managing Historical Computing Projects."

Consortium on Computing for Undergraduate Education

http://www.ccue.org/

This site is dedicated to promoting the improvement of undergraduate teaching through the use of computers. It contains suggestions, discussions, examples, links, and information about the consortium.

Courses On-Line—The Humanities Server

http://human.www.sunet.se/courses/courses.html

This site presents numerous links to sites that sponsor on-line courses and educational initiatives.

Directory of History Departments in the United States and Canada

http://web.gmu.edu/departments/history/research/depts.html

Maintained by George Mason University, this site provides an index of links to all of the history departments in the United States and Canada that have an on-line site.

Distance Educator

http://www.DISTANCE-EDUCATOR.com/

The *Distance Educator* WWW site provides articles about on-line and distance-learning courses as well as an excellent collection of links to related sites.

Distance Learning Laboratory

http://stargate.con-ed.howard.edu/WebPages/dll/

The Distance Learning Laboratory contains articles, links, and forums on the topic.

Ed-Tech

http://h-net2.msu.edu/~edweb/

Ed-Tech is an H-Net–sponsored discussion list. Its Web site contains an archive of all past messages from this group and links to other educational technology sites.

Edupage

http://www.ee.surrey.ac.uk/Contrib/Edupage/

Edupage is published tri-weekly by the University of Surrey. The format consists of short blurbs that cover a broad range of computing, technological, and educational themes.

Eh.student

http://cs.muohio.edu/

Affiliated with H-Net, this is the Web site of the Eh.student discussion list. Eh.student explores issues affecting students and teachers of economic history. The site contains information about the discussion list and allows one to subscribe. It also includes calls for papers, conference announcements, bibliographies, reviews, articles, and links to related sites.

Eh.teach

http://cs.muohio.edu/

Affiliated with H-Net, this is the Web site of the Eh.teach discussion list, which focuses on the teaching of economic history. The site contains information about the discussion list and allows one to subscribe. It also includes syllabi, calls for papers, conference announcements, bibliographies, reviews, articles, and links to related sites.

Global Network Academy: Distance Learning Catalog

http://uu-gna.mit.edu:8001/uu-gna/documents/catalog/index.html

The GNL Meta-Library Search is a search tool that will explore the Web for on-line courses.

H-High-S

http://h-net2.msu.edu/~highs

This site is the Web page of the H-Net–sponsored H-High-S discussion list. H-High-S focuses on all the issues that concern high school teachers of history and social studies. The Web site contains information about the discussion list and allows one to subscribe. It also includes lists of syllabi, suggestions for courses, conference announcements, articles, and links to related sites.

H-Mac

http://polyglot.lss.wisc.edu/hmac/hmachome.html

This is the Web site of the H-Mac discussion list. Supported by H-Net, this group focuses on history and pedagogical software as well as classroom applications for Macintosh computers. Their Web pages contain information about the discussion list and allow one to subscribe. They also include conference announcements, bibliographies, reviews, articles, and links to related sites.

H-Mmedia

http://h-net2.msu.edu/~mmedia

Sponsored by H-Net, this is the Web site of the H-Mmedia discussion list. H-Mmedia focuses on high-tech, multimedia teaching. The site contains information about the discussion list and allows one to subscribe. It also includes syllabi, suggestions for applying multimedia products to the classroom and research, calls for papers, conference announcements, bibliographies, multimedia reviews, articles, and links to related sites.

H-Survey

http://h-net2.msu.edu/~survey

This is the Web site of the H-Survey discussion list. Affiliated with H-Net, this group shares ideas and information for teaching college survey courses in United States history. Their Web pages contain information about the discussion list and allow one to subscribe. They also include syllabi, course suggestions, conference announcements, bibliographies, book reviews, articles, and links to related sites.

H-Teach

http://h-net2.msu.edu/~teach

This is the Web site of the H-Teach discussion list. Affiliated with H-Net, this group shares ideas and information for teaching college history courses. Their Web pages contain information about the discussion list and allow one to subscribe. They also include syllabi, course suggestions, conference announcements, bibliographies, book reviews, articles, and links to related sites.

H-W-civ

http://h-net2.msu.edu/~wciv

This is the Web site of the H-W-civ discussion list. Affiliated with H-Net, this group shares ideas and information for Western civilization courses. Their Web pages contain information about the discussion list and allow one to subscribe. They also include syllabi, course suggestions, conference announcements, bibliographies, book reviews, articles, and links to related sites.

Helping Your Child Learn History—History as Story

http://www.ed.gov:/pubs/parents/History/Story.html

This site, aimed primarily at parents, offers suggestions for bringing history alive. Sponsored by the United States government, its suggestions are equally pertinent for K–12 teachers.

History and Computing

http://grid.let.rug.nl/ahc/journal.html

This site covers a broad range of topics relating to using computers as a methodological and teaching tool for historians.

History and Social Studies Web Site for K–12 Teachers

http://execpc.com/~dboals/boals.html

The History and Social Studies Web Site for K–12 Teachers is an excellent general gateway to resources for teachers.

The History Channel

http://www.historychannel.com

The History Channel's WWW site includes program listings, instructional guides for featured shows, and a host of other materials that teachers, professors, and lovers of history will find useful.

History Education Begins at Home

http://hkein.ie.cuhk.hk/Education/Kids/LearnHistory/Home.html

This site contains an essay on how parents can teach their children history, and it provides a practical list of activities to develop young children's interest in history.

History Fellowships

gopher://gopher.uiuc.edu:70/11/UI/DInfo/History/H-Albion/fellow

This Web page contains information about the application procedures and deadlines for a variety of grants available to historians.

History Happens

http://www.ushistory.com/

This site has a nice beat, and you can teach to it. It is an ambitious attempt to put history to music and presents a collection of videos based on events in American history. Links to other sites as well.

History on Public TV

http://www.current.org/hi1.html

This site provides a frequently updated guide to history programming on public television.

Humanist Discussion Group

http://www.princeton.edu/~mccarty/humanist/humanist.html

This is a forum for discussing the applications of computer technology to the humanities. On-line subscription information available.

Institute for Academic Technology Home Page

http://www.iat.unc.edu/

The Institute for Academic Technology Home Page is dedicated to exploring the vast potential of computer technologies for education. It contains articles, hints, product reviews, and a wide array of related sites.

InterActive Teacher On-Line

http://www.interactiveteacher.com/

InterActive Teacher is an on-line forum that sponsors articles and multimedia presentations related to teaching.

Internet University

http://www.caso.com/iuhome.html

The Internet University provides an extensive list of links to on-line courses in history and other subject areas.

Living Schoolbook Project

http://www.npac.syr.edu/projects/ltb/Glimpse/cover.html

This site is devoted to exploring ways in which technology can be used to improve teaching and learning.

National Standards for History

http://www.sscnet.ucla.edu/nchs/

These are the standards that have been getting so much attention lately. Log in and read them for yourself!

On-Line Books Page

http://www.cs.cmu.edu/Web/books.html

The On-Line Books Page is a comprehensive listing of most repositories of on-line books throughout the world, including many foreign language sites.

PRESED-X, Preservation Educators' Exchange

http://www.well.com/user/bronxbob/presed-x/presed-x.html

PRESED-X is a forum for teachers and professors of preservation. It includes an excellent collection of links to preservation-related education resources.

Preservation Education Directory

http://www.crp.cornell.edu/presdir.html

The Preservation Education Directory is a guide to programs and sites dedicated to historic preservation.

Project Gutenberg Master Index

http://www.w3.org/pub/DataSources/bySubject/Literature/Gutenberg

Project Gutenberg contains a subject index and an alphabetical list of on-line documents and classics in world history and literature.

School Is Dead, Learn in Freedom!

http://pages.prodigy.com/S/C/D/School_is_dead/Learn_in_freedom.html

This irreverently named site provides links to many sites sponsoring on-line courses and distance learning opportunities.

Social Sciences UCLA Page

http://www.sscnet.ucla.edu

The Social Sciences UCLA Page is an excellent starting point for social studies links. It contains hundreds of connections to social science departments, organizations, institutes, and resources.

Social Studies Sources

http://www.halcyon.com/howlevin/social.studies

Aimed at K–12 teachers, this site contains hundreds of links to social studies Web pages.

Speakeasy Cafe: Internet for Educators

http://www.speakeasy.org/educators/history.html

This site presents a large database of links for K–12 educators.

Studying and Teaching History

http://www.tntech.edu/www/acad/hist/study.html

This site aims to create a database of syllabi and suggestions for teachers and students of history. The site accepts materials from contributors and should become a useful forum for discussing the teaching and learning of history.

SyllabusWeb

http://www.syllabus.com/

This site, produced by *Syllabus* magazine, contains articles and information on the application of electronic technologies in education. Subscription information is also available along with related links.

Teaching with Historic Places Home Page

http://www.cr.nps.gov/nr/twhp/home.html

This site provides an innovative description of how teachers can use field trips to historic places to teach broad aspects of history. The site has many good suggestions for educators.

Teaching Materials for Historians

http://grid.let.rug.nl/ahc/teaching.html

This site contains links to educational materials, electronic classroom projects, on-line syllabi, and more.

Teaching On-Line Courses—An On-Line Course

http://www.cybercorp.net/gymv/crs_out/crs_list.html

This clever and straightforward commercial site explains how teachers and professors can use the WWW for their own courses. It offers many suggestions and an introduction to HTML—the language of the Web.

United States Department of Education

http://www.ed.gov/

This is the official home page of the Department of Education. It is an excellent place to learn about federal educational initiatives, and it contains links to related sites. Those who are interested can find the United States history standards and other policy documents on-line at this site.

United States Distance Learning Association Home Page

http://www.usdla.org/

This is the Web presence of the United States Distance Learning Association. It contains information about the organization, lists of on-line and distance courses, and teaching suggestions.

University of California, Berkeley, Teaching Tips

gopher://infocal.berkeley.edu/11/.p/otherdepts/ttips/GD

This site offers teachers and professors a number of suggestions for improving their teaching and interaction with students.

Using the Multimedia Tools of the Internet for Teaching History in K–12 Schools

http://www.xs4all.nl/~swanson/history/index.html

This is a useful site put together by a high school history teacher. It introduces the basics of Web page authoring and provides many suggestions for K–12 teachers. There are also many links to other educational resources.

World Lecture Hall

http://www.utexas.edu:80/world/lecture/

This is a great way to find out how faculty are using the Internet in their college teaching. It is arranged by subject area and presents Web sites for college classes throughout the country, usually including course syllabi, assignments, lecture notes, and multimedia readings.

World Studies Page

http://www.ilt.columbia.edu/k12/livetext/global.html

The World Studies Page contains lesson plans, student projects, on-line activities, and indices to other Internet resources for the study of world history and culture.

DISCUSSION LISTS

Discussion lists are one of the most beneficial resources on the Internet, and one of the most important organizations sponsoring history discussion lists is H-Net—the Humanities On-Line Initiative which is funded by the National Endowment for the Humanities and Michigan State University. H-Net supports nearly one hundred discussion groups covering a wide range of historical topics. The discussion groups supported by H-Net are listed first, followed by those groups that are sponsored by some other organization or institution. To subscribe to one of these lists, you must send what is called a "subscribe message" to the address listed below. A subscribe message contains simply the text listed below followed by your full name. An example is:

Subscribe H-France Jean-Jacques Rousseau

Part one describes subscribing to discussion lists in more detail. The following information gives the addresses of the listservers to which subscription messages should be sent.

H-NET LISTS

For the lists below, send a subscribe message to listserv @uicvm.uic.edu

H-Antis, Anti-Semitism
H-Ideas, Intellectual history
H-Italy, Italian history and culture
H-Urban, Urban history
HOLOCAUS, Holocaust studies
IEAHCnet, Colonial; Seventeenth- and eighteenth-century America

For the following lists, send a subscribe message to listserv@msu.edu

H-Africa, African history
H-Albion, British and Irish history
H-AmRel, American religious history
H-AmStdy, American studies
H-Asia, Asian studies and history
H-Canada, Canadian history and studies
H-CivWar, American Civil War
H-CLC, Comparative literature and computing
H-Demog, Demographic history
H-Diplo, Diplomatic history, international affairs
H-Ethnic, Ethnic, immigration and emigration studies
H-Film, Scholarly studies and uses of media
H-German, German history
H-Grad, Graduate student topics
H-High-S, Teaching high school history/social studies
H-Judaic, Judaica and Jewish history
H-Labor, Labor history
H-LatAm, Latin American history
H-Law, Legal and constitutional history
H-Local, State and local history and museums

H-Mac, Macintosh users
H-MMedia, Discussions of multimedia teaching
H-NZ-OZ, New Zealand and Australian history
H-PCAACA, Popular Culture and American Culture Association
H-Review, Book reviews
H-Rhetor, History of rhetoric and communications
H-Rural, Rural and agricultural history
H-Russia, Russian history
H-SAE, European anthropology
H-SHGAPE, American Gilded Age and Progressive Era
H-South, American South
H-State, Discussions of the welfare state
H-Survey, Teaching United States survey courses
H-State, Discussions of the welfare state
H-Teach, Teaching college history
H-W-Civ, Teaching Western civilization
H-West, United States West, frontiers
H-Women, Women's history
H-World, World history

For the lists below, send a subscribe message to listserv @ksuvm. ksu.edu

H-Pol, American politics
H-War, Military history

For the following lists, a subscribe message should be sent to listserv@vm.cc.purdue.edu

H-France, French history
Habsburg, Austro-Hungarian Empire

For LPBR-L, send a subscribe message to listserv @listserv.acns. nwu. edu

LPBR-L, Law and politics book review

For H-Mexico, send a subscribe message to h-mexico@servidor.
unam.mx

H-MEXICO, Mexican history and studies

For the lists below, send a subscribe message to
lists@cs.muohio.edu

EH.RES, Economic history short research notes and queries
EH.DISC, Economic history extended discussion
EH.NEWS, Economic history news, announcements
EconHist.Macro, Macroeconomic history, business cycles
Eh.eastbloc, Economic history of Eastern Europe
EconHist.Student, Students and faculty in economic history
EconHist.Teach, Teaching economic history
Global.change, Historical dimensions of global change
H-Business, Business history
Quanhist.recurrent, Comparative recurrent phenomena

OTHER DISCUSSION LISTS

AERA-F, Educational history and historiography
Send a "subscribe AERA-F" message to listserv@asuvm.inre.asu.edu

AEROSP-L, Aeronautical and aerospace history
Send a "subscribe AEROSP-L" message to listserv@sivm.si.edu

AMERCATH, History of American Catholicism
Send a "subscribe AMERCATH" message to listserv@lsv.uky.edu

ANCIEN-L, Ancient history
Send a "suscribe ANCIEN-L" message to listserv%ulkyvm.
bitnet@listserv.net

ASHR-L, American Society for the History of Rhetoric
Send a "subscribe ASHR-L" message to listserv@psuvm.psu.edu

ASTR-L, Theater history
Send a "subscribe ASTR-L" message to listserv@postoffice.cso. uiuc.edu

AZTLAN, Pre-Columbian history
Send a "subscribe AZTLAN" message to listserv%ulkyvm.bitnet @listserv.net

CAAH, Consortium of Art and Architectural Historians
Send a "subscribe CAAH" message to listserv@pucc.princeton.edu

C18-L, Eighteenth-century interdisciplinary studies
Send a "subscribe C18-L" message to listserv@psuvm.edu

CHA-97, Canadian Historical Association 1997
Send a "subscribe CHA-97" message to listserv@morgan.ucs.mun.ca

CHEIRON, Society for the History of the Social and Behavioral Sciences
Send a "subscribe CHEIRON" message to listserv@yorku.ca

COMHIST, History of human communication
Send a "subscribe COMHIST" message to listserv@vm.its.rpi.edu

CPN, Canadian History of Psychology Network
Send a "subscribe CPN-HISTORY-OF-PSYCHOLOGY" message to listserv@listserv.nodak.edu

EARLYSCIENCE-L, History of Science Society, Early Science Interest Group
Send a "subscribe EARLYSCIENCE-L" message to listserv@listserv. vt.edu

EHCOLUMN, *Economic History Columns*
Send a "subscribe EHCOLUMN" message to listserv@miamiu. muohio.edu

ELIAS-I, Figurational studies in social science, history, and psychology
Send a "subscribe ELIAS-I" message to listserv@nic.surfnet.nl

ESPORA-L, History of the Iberian Peninsula
Send a "subscribe ESPORA-L" message to listserv@ukanvm.cc.ukans.edu

ETHNOHIS, Ethnology and history
Send a "subscribe ETHNOHIS" message to listserv@nic.surfnet.nl

HASTRO-L, History of astronomy
Send a "subscribe HASTRO-L" message to listserv@wvnvm.wvnet.edu

HISLAW-L, Legal history
Send a "subscribe HISLAW-L" message to listserv%ulkyvm.bitnet@listserv.ne

HIST-L, All historical topics
Send a "subscribe HIST-L" message to listserv@ukanvm.cc.ukans.edu

HISTARCH, Historical archaeology
Send a "subscribe HISTARCH" message to listserv@asuvm.inre.asu.edu

HISTNEWS, Historians' newsletter, professional themes
Send a "subscribe HISTNEWS" message to listserv@ukanvm.cc.ukans.edu

HISTORY, All historical topics
Send a "subscribe HISTORY" message to listserv@irlearn.ucd.ie

HISTOWNR, Sponsors of history-related lists
Send a "subscribe HISTOWNR" message to listserv@ubvm.cc.buffalo.edu

HOPOS-L, History of the philosophy of science
Send a "subscribe HOPOS-L" message to listserv@lsv.uky.edu

HPSST-L, History and philosophy of science and science teaching
Send a "subscribe HPSST-L" message to listserv@qucdn.queensu.ca

HTECH-L, History of technology
Send a "subscribe HTECH-L" message to listserv@sivm.si.edu

ISLAM-L, History of Islam
Send a "subscribe ISLAM-L" message to listserv%ulkyvm.bitnet@ listserv.net

JSH, *Journal of Southern History*
Send a "subscribe JSH" message to listserv@ricevm1.rice.edu

MAPHIST, Map history
Send a "subscribe MAPHIST" message to listserv%harvarda.bitnet @listserv.net

MEDART-L, Medieval art history
Send a "subscribe MEDART-L" message to listserv@listserv. utoronto.ca

MEDIEV-L, Medieval history
Send a "subscribe MEDIEV-L" message to listserv@ukanvm.cc. ukans.edu

MENA-H, History of the Middle East and North Africa
Send a "subscribe MENA-H" message to listserv%ulkyvm.bitnet@ listserv.net

MILHST-L, Military history
Send a "subscribe MILHST-L" message to listserv@ukanvm.cc. ukans.edu

MISSIONS, Missionary history
Send a "subscribe MISSIONS" message to listserv@yalevm.cis. yale.edu

OHA-L, Oral History Association
Send a "subscribe OHA-L" message to listserv@lsv.uky.edu

PHILOFHI-L, Philosophy of history
Send a "subscribe PHILOFHI-L" message tolistserv@yorku.ca

PUBLHIST, Public history
Send a "subscribe PUBLHIST" message to listserv@listserv.iupui.edu

RENAIS-L, Renaissance history
Send a "subscribe RENAIS-L" message to listserv%ulkyvm.
bitnet@listserv.net

SAH-L, Society of Architectural Historians
Send a "subscribe SAH-L" message to listserv@sivm.si.edu

SHARP-L, Society for the History of Authorship, Reading, and Publishing
Send a "subscribe SHARP-L" message to listserv@iubvm.ucs.indiana.edu

SHOTHC-L, Computer history
Send a "subscribe SHOTHC-L" message to listserv@sivm.si.edu

SISTER-L, History of female Catholic religious
Send a "subscribe SISTER-L" message to listserv@listserv.syr.edu

SLAVERY, History of slavery
Send a "subscribe SLAVERY" message to listserv@listserv.uh.edu

SPORTHIST, Sports history
Send a "subscribe SPORTHIST" message to listserv@pdomain.
uwindsor.ca

STUDIUM, University history
Send a "subscribe STUDIUM" message to listserv@cc1.kuleuven.
ac.be

SWCLIO, History of American education
Send a "subscribe SWCLIO" message to listserv@tamvm1.tamu.edu

TAMHA, Teaching American history
Send a "subscribe TAMHA" message to listserv@cms.cc.wayne.edu

TARIKH-L, Iranian history
Send a "subscribe TARIKH-L" message to listserv@yalevm.cis. yale.edu

WHIRL, Women's history in rhetoric and language
Send a "subscribe WHIRL" message to listserv@psuvm.psu.edu

WOMHIST, Women's history
Send a "subscribe WOMHIST" message to listserv@vm.temple.edu

WORLD-L, World history
Send a "subscribe WORLD-L" message to listserv@ubvm.cc.buf-falo.edu

---

NEWSGROUPS (USENET GROUPS)

Like discussion lists, newsgroups are an interesting and enjoyable way to engage in a discussion or learn about your favorite historical topics. The addresses of newsgroups are simple to remember. They are the name of the group plus the tag news://. For example, to have your browser bring up the soc.history.living group, you would type

news://soc.history.living.

A complete list of the more than ten thousand newsgroups is accessible on line at:

UseNet News Groups: Comprehensive Directory
http://www.tile.net/tile/news/index.html

The following groups are likely to be of particular interest to readers of *The History Highway:*

alt.history.living—History and reenactments.
alt.history.ocean-liners.titanic—The history of ocean-liners.
alt.history.what-if—What-if scenarios in history.
soc.college—A general forum on college issues.
soc.college.teaching-asst—Issues affecting TAs.
soc.history—A wide array of historical topics.
soc.history.living—Living history and reenactment.
soc.history.medieval—Medieval topics.
soc.history.moderated—All aspects of history.
soc.history.science—History of science.
soc.history.war—All wars and military history.
soc.history.war.misc—Military history.
soc.history.war.us-civil-war—Aspects of the U.S. Civil War.
soc.history.war.vietnam—The Vietnam War.
soc.history.war.world-war-ii—World War II and the Holocaust.
soc.libraries—Library issues.

ELECTRONIC JOURNALS

One of the more exciting historical resources available on the Internet is the on-line journal. The electronic medium offers interesting benefits over traditional print journals, such as nearly unlimited space and the use of hyper-links to connect to other sites. Some long-established journals are expanding or are already on the Internet, while many more are starting from scratch. At this time, there are about a dozen on-line history journals and scholarly newsletters, and in the next year this number should increase to around fifty or more.

Aestel: Medieval and Renaissance Studies

http://weber.u.washington.edu/~mcnelis/AEstelindex.html

Aestel is a relatively new historical and literary journal published by graduate students from the University of Washington. This endeavor is geared toward current trends in medieval literary criticism.

American Studies Association Newsletter

http://www.georgetown.edu/crossroads/asanews/asanews.html

Sponsored by the Society for American Studies, *Connections* contains announcements, job listings, calls for papers, and other forms of communications for the society. There are also many links to related materials.

Ancient History Bulletin

http://137.122.12.15/Docs/Directories/AHB/AHB.html

Published in English, Spanish, Italian, and German. The *Ancient History Bulletin* is devoted to short articles and notes in the field of ancient history and ancillary fields such as numismatics. Scholarly discourse is encouraged, and articles are accepted over the Internet for publication.

Arachnion: A Journal of Literature and Ancient History on the Web

http://www.cisi.unito.it/arachne/arachne.html

Published in Italy at the University of Bologna, *Arachnion* is an online journal that features articles and forums on the ancient world. There are also announcements and many useful links to related sites.

The Association for Asian Studies Newsletter

http://bbanning.memorial.indiana.edu/~aas/

The Association for Asian Studies Newsletter is issued five times a year and includes notices of fellowships, grants, and conferences, as well as a job placement registry and information from the secretariat. It also includes a directory of electronic journals, newsletters, and academic discussion lists. A standard for those interested in Asian history.

The Bryn Mawr Classical Review

gopher://gopher.lib.Virginia.edu:70/11/alpha/bmcr

The Bryn Mawr Classical Review is a monthly journal published jointly by Bryn Mawr College and the University of Pennsylvania. It contains reviews of books on Greek and Latin literature and history and has occasional notices (e.g., about conferences). It has an excellent archive of past articles and reviews that is searchable by author, reviewer, or book title. Located only in gopher (non-graphic) format, it has been on-line since 1990, and, like its sister publication The *Bryn Mawr Medieval Review,* there are plans to put it on the World Wide Web.

The Bryn Mawr Medieval Review

gopher://gopher.lib.Virginia.edu:70/11/alpha/bmmr

The Bryn Mawr Medieval Review is edited out of the University of Washington in conjunction with Bryn Mawr College. It publishes timely reviews of current work in all areas of medieval studies, a field it interprets as broadly as possible (chronologically, geographically, and culturally). The journal's editors are eager to develop a large and diverse stable of reviewers who will offer broad coverage of interesting current work from all over the world. Although currently available only in gopher (non-graphic) format, there are plans to put it on to the World Wide Web. The editorial board consists of influential scholars in the field, including Patrick Geary (UCLA) and Robert Stacey (University of Washington). Both the *Bryn Mawr Classical* and *Medieval Reviews* have very open copyright policies.

Chronicon

http://www.ucc.ie/chronicon/

Chronicon is an electronic journal of international history published by the Department of History at University College, Cork, Ireland. It is envisaged that the journal will appear twice yearly beginning in spring 1996, and it will publish articles relating to history from the post-classical period to contemporary history. Articles will be peer reviewed. It will contain reviews of publications and notices of scholarly developments in the field of history. The journal will provide a forum for scholars to exchange views on matters of topical interest. Currently a test site is up and running.

Classics Ireland

http://www.ucd.ie/~classics/ClassIre95.html

The Journal of the Classical Association of Ireland publishes articles and reviews on the classics, ancient history, and archaeology. The current issue has an interesting article by rock musician Iggy Pop, who explains how he came to write the track "Caesar" on his latest album *American Caesar*. While not a "scholarly" article, it nonetheless is illustrative of how electronic journals are reaching a much broader audience.

CLIONET: The Australian Electronic Journal of History

gopher://marlin.jcu.edu.au:70/

An electronic journal-network affiliated with H-Net, CLIONET maintains a gopher site of scholarship and documents relating to the history of Australasia and publishes new work in Australian and related historical fields. *CLIONET* is located on the gopher site "Academic Departments" at James Cook University of North Queensland.

Comitatus: A Journal of Medieval and Renaissance Studies

http://www.humnet.ucla.edu/humnet/cmrs/publications/comitatus/com itatu.htm

Comitatus is a journal that aims to publish the work of new medieval scholars. Submission and subscription information is included. The site also includes a table of contents to all previous issues, subscription information, and links to related sites.

The Concord Review

http://www.tcr.org/

This publication features the work of secondary school students in history. It claims to be the only publication of its kind in the United States. Information on its history, subscriptions, and sample essays are provided, along with a recent table of contents. Essays topics range from the "Great Awakening" to "Woodrow Wilson," from the "Negro Leagues" to the "Union Blockade."

Electronic Antiquity: Communicating the Classics

gopher://babel.its.utas.edu.au:70/11/Publications/Electronic%20Antiq
uity%20%3A%20Communicating%20The%20Classics

This is a monthly newsletter published out of the University of Tasmania, Australia, which deals with ancient history and archaeology. It is a refereed, international journal that publishes scholarly articles and reviews, as well as "kite-flying" papers seeking feedback and items of interest (announcements of conferences and vacant positions) to the wider classics community. It has been on-line since June 1993 and is currently available only on gopher. It is unknown when it will be put on the World Wide Web, but it certainly has the longest URL we have ever seen.

Essays in History

http://www.lib.virginia.edu/journals/EH/EH.html

Essays in History is a refereed journal published annually for the past thirty-five years by graduate students of the Corcoran Department of History at the University of Virginia. On-line since 1994, it now appears only in electronic form. Each issue has approximately six to eight scholarly journal articles in a wide variety of fields. The current issue (volume 36) contains articles on the medieval period, nineteenth-century Britain and France, Leo Amery's role in World War I, and Thomas Jefferson.

Exemplaria: Medieval and Renaissance Studies

http://www.clas.ufl.edu/english/exemplaria/

Exemplaria is dedicated to contemporary interpretations of medieval literature. Gender roles receive special attention.

Film-Historia

http://www.swcp.com/~cmora/historia.html

Film-Historia is a new journal published in English, Spanish, and Catalán. Its focus is on the interpretation of films in regard to society and culture and on the use of films as tools for teaching history.

Heritage, A Canadian History Magazine

http://heritage.excite.sfu.ca/hpost.html

Heritage is an interactive site for items related to Canadian history and culture.

Historical Gazette: The American Old West

http://www.aracnet.com/~histgaz/

A series of short articles related primarily to Oregon and its role in the West. The *Gazette* also publishes some articles from late-nineteenth-century and early-twentieth-century newspapers in their original form.

History of Australian Science Newsletter

http://www.asap.unimelb.edu.au/hasn/hasn_inf.htm

This is the official newsletter of the Australian Society for the History of Science. The newsletter is released in both print and electronic form, but the electronic version contains the full text, which includes reports, announcements, and calls for papers.

History Reviews On-Line

http://www.uc.edu/www/history/reviews.htmlx

This quarterly on-line journal sponsored by the University of Cincinnati is dedicated to publishing scholarly book reviews of the latest historical works within three months of publication. The editors plan to increase the number of reviews to 150–300 per issue.

History and Theory

http://www.wesleyan.edu/histjrnl/hthome.htm

History and Theory is a journal published by Wesleyan University and contains articles, review essays, and summaries of books principally in the following areas: critical philosophy of history, speculative philosophy of history, historiography, historical methodology, critical theory, time and culture, and related disciplines. At present, *History and Theory*'s Web site offers only subscription information for the journal.

IOUDAIOS Review

http://www.lehigh.edu/lists/ioudaios-review/

IOUDAIOS Review is a quarterly journal for professional scholars of early Judaism and related fields and was spawned by the listserv discussion group IOUDAIOS-L. It is primarily intended to serve professional scholars of early Judaism and related fields, so some knowledge of classical Hebrew and Hellenistic Greek is assumed. It is intended to disseminate information on conferences and publish reviews of pertinent literature. There is an archive of all past issues with a fully cross-referenced bibliographic index. There is also a guide that gives instructions for contributors and supplies transliteration tables for Greek and Hebrew text.

Jewish Studies Judaica E-Journal

gopher://israel.nysernet.org:70/11/ajs/jsej

Jewish Studies Judaica E-Journal is an Internet journal devoted to ongoing research and current events in Jewish studies. It contains short articles, book reviews, collaboration requests, job postings, and conference calls. *JSJEJ* is published by the Israel Project of the New York State Educational Research and the H-Net Project of the University of Illinois-Chicago.

Johns Hopkins TOC of History Journals

gopher://jhunix.hcf.jhu.edu:10003/11/JHU_Press/.zjournals/.hist

This is a journal that catalogs in a searchable index the tables of contents of many current print journals. Currently, it is available only in gopher format, and there are many journals not listed in its tables of contents.

Journal of Material Culture

http://www.sageltd.co.uk/journals/details/mcu.html

Published by Sage, *Journal of Material Culture* is a new interdisciplinary periodical. The on-line version contains only the journal's table of contents and selected articles. Subscription and contribution information is also provided along with a history of the journal.

KMT: A Modern Journal of Ancient Egypt

http://www.sirius.com/~reeder/kmt.html

Created in 1990, *KMT* is an English-language journal published quarterly in Egypt. The title of the journal *KMT* is an abbreviation of Kemet, meaning Black Country, which is what the ancient Egyptians called their homeland. Readers can find the full text of *KMT*'s articles, announcements, reports, and reviews on-line.

Latin American Economic History Newsletter

http://milkman.cac.psu.edu/histrlst/specproj/lamer/laehn

Latin American Economic History Newsletter is produced under the auspices of the Committee on Population and Quantitative History of the Conference on Latin American History, with support from the Penn State Department of History. It publishes essays and reviews, along with information about conferences, fellowships, grants, archives, and databases. Essays and announcements are in English, Spanish, Portuguese, or French. Past issues starting from 1991 are available on-line.

MERGER: Newsletter of the Migration and Ethnic Relations Group for European Research

http://www.ruu.nl/ercomer/merger/index.html

As its title indicates, *MERGER* is the newsletter for the Migration and Ethnic Relations Group for European Research. It is published three times a year, and the on-line version contains the full text of the newsletter.

NewJour

http://gort.ucsd.edu/newjour/

NewJour is a frequently updated database which lists new on-line journals and their addresses as they appear. It is a place to watch for new journals on topics that interest you.

Nineteenth-Century Studies

http://www.fandm.edu/Departments/English/Ohara/19thCStudies.html

Sponsored by the Society for Nineteenth-Century Studies, this site lists the table of contents for the society's yearly publication along with information on how to join the society and how to subscribe or contribute to the journal.

Old World Archaeology Newsletter

http://www.wesleyan.edu/classics/OWAN.html

Old World Archaeology Newsletter (*OWAN*) is published three times a year by the Department of Classical Studies at Wesleyan University, Middletown, Connecticut. It is in the process of creating an archive for current and back issues of the *OWAN* and other resources. Currently there is a limited archive of recent issues.

On-Line Archaeology

http://avebury.arch.soton.ac.uk/Journal/journal.html

A new journal published out of the University of Southampton, UK, *On-Line Archaeology* is a formal, refereed electronic publication with the aim of promoting rapid dissemination of speculative ideas about archaeology and ancient history.

Postmodern Culture Journal

http://ernie.bgsu.edu/~swilbur/PMC_MOO.html

Postmodern Culture is an interdisciplinary e-journal produced under the auspices of the University of Virginia and the Institute for Advanced Technology in the Humanities. Unlike other journals, it is published and revised in a free-flowing and experimental manner. It contains articles, musings, and other types of imaginative scholarly exchange. A truly postmodern journal of cultural studies.

Project Muse

http://muse.mse.jhu.edu/

Project Muse is the National Endowment for the Humanities–sponsored project to make the Johns Hopkins journals available on-line. At present, the full text of more than forty journals in the humanities and sciences are on-line, including *Eighteenth-Century Studies, Bulletin of the History of Medicine, French Historical Studies, Modernism/Modernity, New Literary History* and *Reviews in American History.* Access to the full-text issues is limited to those affiliated with subscribed institutions, but bibliographic material and tables of contents are freely accessible for all the journals.

Scholarly Journals Distributed Via the World Wide Web

http://info.lib.uh.edu/wj/webjour.html

This is an excellent catalog of on-line scholarly journals.

The Slavic Review

http://ccat.sas.upenn.edu/slavrev/slavrev.html

Published quarterly by the University of Pennsylvania's Center for Eastern European and Russian scholars, *The Slavic Review* has been on-line since 1994, making it one of the first Internet journals. While *The Slavic Review* does not offer a full version on-line, it does offer all of the journal articles for each issue. The only major omission is the lack of book reviews, an editorial decision stemming from the belief that book reviews were among the major benefits of subscribing to the print version. *The Slavic Review* is a model for an established journal that is seeking to expand to the Internet for both publicity reasons and as an added resource for historians. As it slowly builds up an archive of past articles, this site will increase in both use and importance.

South Asia Graduate Research Journal

http://asnic.utexas.edu/asnic/sagar/sagar.main.html

This graduate student e-journal publishes the work of young scholars and graduate students in Asian studies. It is supported by the Center for Asian Studies at the University of Texas.

The Southern Register

http://imp.cssc.olemiss.edu/register/95/spring/index.html

The Southern Register is the official newsletter of the Center for the Study of Southern Culture. Published four times a year, the on-line version contains the full contents of the print journal, including articles, reviews, forums, and announcements.

Thematica

http://www.prairienet.org/thematica/

Thematica is an annual journal edited by graduate students at the University of Illinois. It publishes historical articles, reviews, and essays on a given theme. There is an archive of past issues on-line.

Time and Writing

http://www-azc.uam.mx/tye/indice-in.html

Time and Writing is a new (July 1996) journal dedicated to Mexican history. The first issue contains articles on recent trends in research and a number of reviews.

LIBRARIES, ARCHIVES, AND MUSEUMS

USING ON-LINE CATALOGS

When you log into a remote catalog on the Internet, chances are good that the screen you see will be different from the one you are accustomed to encountering in your local library. There are a number of different library menu formats, with varying degrees of difficulty and unique searching techniques. They are generally user-friendly. A good rule of thumb when using library catalogs is to keep your eye on the bottom of the screen for commands. You do not need to memorize the searching techniques of each system, but be aware of where the commands are. As with any site you access on the Internet, pay attention to the commands the system gives you when you log in. The first screen will often be the only screen that gives you the proper entrance and exit instructions, and these will be different for each system.

When you log into a library catalog on the Internet, you will often see additional options on the initial screen. You may see options for outstanding periodical databases such as Lexis/Nexis, Medline, or InfoTrac. You will almost never be able to access these. Libraries must buy access to these products, and their contracts strictly limit their use to their own faculty, students, or local users. After all, how would InfoTrac stay in business if the whole country could log into the New York Public Library and use it free of charge? Save yourself the frustration and do not try to access these resources. All libraries have built in a number of safeguards to insure that unauthorized users cannot access them. The only resource you will generally be allowed to use is the library catalog—the actual book holdings of the library.

Library of Congress

http://lcweb.loc.gov

telnet://locis.loc.gov

The Library of Congress is the world's largest library. The primary mission of the Library of Congress remains meeting the research needs of Congress, and it is these needs that guide the selection of new materials. The needs and interests of Congress are wide and varied, however. After all, this is where a representative would go to learn about the validity of global warming theories, justification for all-day kindergarten, the plight of Alaskan fishermen, or the worthiness of Cole Porter to appear on the next commemorative postal stamp. Granted, it may sometimes appear as if there is no end to the minutiae that Congress is interested in, but there are limits to what the Library of Congress will collect.

Contrary to the commonly held belief, the Library of Congress does *not* own copies of all books published in the United States. For example, you will not find a very good cookbook, comic book, or pulp fiction selection at the Library of Congress. Nevertheless, it is still considered the best library in the world, and it houses the definitive collection of resources for many areas of history. It is open to anyone who wishes to make use of its holdings, either in person or on-line.

There are currently more than 104 million records cataloged in the Library of Congress. Current holdings include:

16,055,353 monographs
43,226,412 manuscripts
4,247,049 maps
16,597,335 visual materials (photographs, etchings, and videos)

This is too large a collection to search in one database. They have divided the collection into the following files for faster searching. You will see these selections on the first screen of the catalog. Simply type the desired name to access the database.

Type of Item	File Name
Books cataloged since 1968	LOCI
Books cataloged prior to 1968	PREM
Serials cataloged after 1973	LOCS
Maps and other cartographic items cataloged after 1968	LOCM

Please note that when they say an item was "cataloged" after a certain date, this does not refer to the date it was published. It refers to the date that the record for that item was formally processed by the library. For example, if the library bought a copy of *Huckleberry Finn* in 1975, you would search the LOCI file for this volume. If you needed to locate the record of the original copy that the Library of Congress bought in 1884, you would need to search the PREM file.

Accessing the catalog of the Library of Congress is very easy. Unfortunately, everything gets more difficult from there. The first thing you need to be aware of is that unlike almost all other sites on the Internet, access to the Library of Congress catalog is available only during the following hours (Eastern Standard Time): Monday–Friday 6:30 A.M.–9:30 P.M., Saturday 8:00 A.M.–5:00 P.M., and Sunday 1:00 P.M.–5:00 P.M.

The catalog itself is called LOCIS (Library of Congress On-Line System) and is not very easy for the novice to navigate. Developed in the early 1970s, it was one of the first computerized library catalogs in the world. It was developed with librarians and catalogers in mind, not the typical searcher. Be prepared for a little frustration when you first begin your research. Still, it is not rocket science, and this may be your best bet for many resources. The Library of Congress knows that the system is user unfriendly and talks about making changes someday. In the meantime, here are some tips on searching the catalog.

Most searches initially begin with a **browse** command (which can be shortened to a **b**):

> Author search:
> b boorstin, daniel
> Title search:
> b mask of command
> Subject search:
> b agriculture—soil erosion—history

A Note About Subject Searching: In order to do effective subject searching in this database, you must make use of Library of Congress subject headings. If you do not know the correct subject heading, you should use the command Keyword Search: to find key words for your topic. For example:

> Keyword Search:
> find farming and soil erosion

After you enter your search, you will be presented with an alphabetical index of topics that closely match your request. Select the line number that matches your search with the command s, followed by the appropriate line number. For example:

> s b6

At some point in your searching you may begin to accumulate "sets" of information. The command to display these is

> d 1 (or the appropriate set number)

You can e-mail reference questions to lcon-line@seq1.loc.gov. They can answer questions about using the Library of Congress catalog or other general reference questions that cannot be answered by your local university library.

OHIOLINK

telnet://cat.ohiolink.edu

When asked for a username/password, type: Ohiolink

This is one of the most useful library catalogs you can access over the Internet. This database provides access to the shared catalogs of over thirty college and university libraries from the state of Ohio. When you log into the catalog, you are searching all thirty library catalogs *simultaneously*. The combined strength of these libraries yields an impressive collection. One of the best things about OhioLink is its ease of use. The interface is as easy as any catalog you will find. For scholars who want extensive research, this is usually a better starting point than the Library of Congress. The size and ease of use in OhioLink will allow more detailed and precise searching than you are likely to find at the Library of Congress. If you have exhausted the OhioLink catalog and still need additional research, *then* go to the Library of Congress or another specialized catalog.

Melvyl

telnet://melvyl.ucop.edu

Melvyl is the catalog of the University of California and the California State Library. As with other joint catalogs, it has access to vast holdings, currently more than eight million titles. Although not as easy to use as OhioLink, if you are interested in Californian, Western, or Hispanic history, this may be a more complete catalog.

Presidential Libraries

http://www.yahoo.com/Reference/Libraries/Presidential£ibraries/

http://sunsite.unc.edu:80/lia/president

In 1939, legislation was passed which decreed that the papers of the presidents would be made available to the public. The term "papers of the president" is very broad. It includes letters, calendars, drafts of legislation, diplomatic communications, transcripts of speeches, and interviews. It may also include the papers of the first lady, cabinet members, and other close associates of the president. The locations of presidential libraries are decided entirely by the former president. This explains why Carter's library is in Atlanta, Georgia, Reagan's library is in Simi Valley, California, and Bush's library is being built in College Station, Texas.

Many items in the presidential libraries are donated, and the Freedom of Information Act *does not* apply to donated personal papers, so you will not have access to everything. Items classified for national security reasons are also unavailable to the public. The Freedom of Information Act does apply to any of the federal records contained in the libraries, and these will be available to anyone. General holdings of the presidential libraries are open to any interested person, although you may need to make advance arrangements in some cases. Check the gopher for the requirements at specific libraries.

At this point, the advantage of Internet access is its ability to give you insight into the nature of the papers each presidential library holds. There is little definitive research that can be done entirely on-line, although most of the libraries are willing to provide limited reference service via e-mail.

You can browse the collection of many of these libraries on-line. The following presidential libraries have Internet sites: Franklin Roosevelt, Eisenhower, Johnson, Nixon, Ford, Carter, and Reagan. Although there are no searchable databases you can log into, most of them do a fairly good job of describing the kind of collection they have. (For example, the file may say, "Seventeen linear feet of documents pertaining to the presidential commission on mental health.")

CRL: The Center for Research Libraries

telnet://crlcatalog.uchicago.edu

When asked for a username/password, type: guest

The Center for Research Libraries is a project devoted to the preservation of rare research materials. In the 1940s, scholars and librarians were becoming concerned over the alarming number of research materials that were being lost, either through physical deterioration or simply because materials were being discarded when they reached a certain age and were deemed obsolete. Recognizing that many of these materials were still of interest to scholars, the Center for Research libraries was established in Chicago in 1949. It is supported by dues paid by the 130 colleges and universities that belong to the consortium.

This may be a good catalog to investigate if you suspect that there has been research done on your topic in the past, but you have been unable to locate it in traditional libraries. Their catalog is very easy to use, and you may uncover some long-lost gems.

In addition to older materials, CRL has a certain amount of foreign research that is not actively being collected by other libraries. They currently own more than 150,000 serial and monographic titles issued by foreign governments, with special emphasis on Southeast Asia. Foreign newspapers and ethnic newspapers from the United States are also acquired. The collection currently has more than three million volumes of research materials that are rarely held by American libraries.

CARL Uncover

telnet://database.carl.org

CARL Uncover is a service that provides access to the tables of contents for more than 17,000 journals in all fields. CARL Uncover is updated daily and is therefore more current than typical computer indexes, which are generally updated four times a year. CARL Uncover can also be used to help you identify journals that may be interested in publishing your research.

CARL Uncover is a for-profit service, but you have free access to its catalog. When you first access CARL Uncover, you will be presented with a screen of cryptic options. You will want to select "#1 Uncover—Article Access and Document Delivery." Do not be intimidated by all the initial messages that ask you to "enter your account number here." At such screens, your last option is always "press enter to continue without an account." You will go through four or five screens of this nature before you are logged into the catalog.

CARL Uncover supports itself by faxing or sending customers the full text of journal articles. If you choose to purchase an article, it will cost you approximately $8.50 per article, plus royalty fees. They promise faxing delivery within 24 hours. There is no obligation to order any articles, and you have unlimited browsing privileges in the catalog.

CARL Uncover can also provide a current awareness service, in which they will e-mail you the table of contents for the journals you have requested each month. The service is rather expensive, however, so remember, you *can* log into the catalog and do the same thing yourself for free, if you have the discipline to remember each month!

The American Antiquarian Society

telnet://mark.mwa.org

gopher://mark.mwa.org

The American Antiquarian Society (AAS) was founded in 1812 and is located in Worcester, Massachusetts. It is in the process of collecting and preserving all printed source material produced in this country before 1877. Those items that cannot be obtained by the AAS will still have their records added into their database, making this catalog an outstanding source to consult for research relating to American history. To date, the collection contains nearly three million items, including books, pamphlets, broadsides, newspapers, children's literature, and maps. It currently owns two-thirds of the total pieces known to have been printed in this country between 1640 and 1821. The AAS has one of the best collections of American eighteenth- and nineteenth-century newspapers in the world, with more than two million issues of such papers.

The AAS on-line catalog is a work in progress. The entire collection is not yet loaded into the database, although the pre-1801 collection is fairly complete. The record for each item will indicate other libraries that also own copies of that item. The system is a little awkward to get used to, but they have some outstanding help screens to get you started. You may want to make some printouts of these before you delve in.

National Archives and Records Administration

http://www.nara.gov/

gopher://gopher.nara.gov/

The National Archives and Records Administration (NARA) is a branch of the government that makes available the records of enduring value from the legislative, executive, and judicial branches of the federal government. The actual archives are located in Washington, D.C., although a new facility is being built in College Park, Maryland. Eventually, the bulk of the collection will be housed in the College Park location. The holdings at NARA come in many forms, including loose papers, microfilm, electronic records, bound volumes, maps, and photographs. NARA claims to have holdings of more than four *billion* items. This is a mind-boggling number, but considering the profusion of documentation pouring out of Congress and all other governmental bodies each day, and that NARA tries to collect everything the government has produced since 1774, this number becomes a little more conceivable. Unfortunately, the huge size of the collection means that an on-line catalog is still many years away, but the Internet site still contains valuable information.

The NARA Internet site gives you a good idea of the types of materials they collect. They maintain an extensive collection of genealogical materials, including immigrant passenger lists, census records, military service records, and federal court records. Although you will be unable to access the actual records via the Internet, you may be able to identify the specific microfilm rolls you need. You can then check to see if a library near you owns a copy of the microfilm or arrange for an interlibrary loan from NARA.

TOP TEN RESEARCH LIBRARIES IN THE UNITED STATES

Although it is always dangerous to evaluate a library based on a numerical count of its holdings, it is probably the most relied-upon measure. The following is a listing of the largest United States research libraries and their Internet addresses:

Harvard University
telnet://hollis.harvard.edu

Yale University
telnet://130.132.21.133

University of California, Berkeley
telnet://gladis.berkeley.edu/

University of California, Los Angeles
telnet://melvyl.ucop.edu:23/

Columbia University
telnet://columbianet.columbia.edu

University of Texas
telnet://utxuts.dp.utexas.edu

Stanford University
telnet://forsythetn.stanford.edu

Cornell University
telnet://ez-cornellc.cit.cornell.edu

University of Michigan
telnet://mirlyn.Telnet.lib.umich.edu

University of Washington
telnet://uwcat.lib.washington.edu

EUROPEAN LIBRARIES

An easy to use Web page for navigating European libraries, complete with passwords and entrance instructions, can be found at:

http://portico.bl.uk/gabriel/en/welcome.html

SPECIAL COLLECTIONS

Just as a museum may have an interest in developing an exceptional art collection in a particular area, such as medieval manuscripts or Egyptian sculpture, libraries may also develop specialties. Often this is to support a particular degree program the university is offering. It may also be the result of historical accident (the Boston Public Library is probably still the best place to get research on the Boston Tea Party), or it could be due to a large gift from a private collection that the library received. Below are the names and addresses of several important libraries that are noted for particular historical collections:

African-American Studies

Howard University: telnet://humaina.howard.edu

New York Public Library: telnet://nyplgate.nypl.org

State University of New York, Buffalo: telnet://snybufvb.cs.snybuf.edu

American Colonial History

Harvard: telnet://hollis.harvard.edu

University of Virginia: telnet://ublan.acc.virginia.edu

Ancient History

Princeton University: telnet://catalog.princeton.edu

Duke University: telnet://ducatalog.lib.duke.edu

Archaeology

Boston University: telnet://library.bu.edu

University of California, Berkeley: telnet://gopac.berkeley.edu

Asian and Pacific Studies

Cornell: telnet://ez-cornellc.cit.cornell.edu

Feminism

Northwestern University: tn3270://library.ucc.nmu.edu

Folklore

Indiana University: telnet://iuis.ucs.indiana.edu

Cleveland Public Library: telnet://library.cpl.org

History of Science and Medicine

Johns Hopkins University: telnet://janus-gate.mse.jhu.edu

Indiana University: telnet://iuis.ucs.indiana.edu

Judaica

University of Florida (Gainesville): telnet://luis.nerdc.ufl.edu

New York Public Library: telnet://nyplgate.nypl.org

Labor and Trade Unions

Johns Hopkins University: telnet://janus-gate.mse.jhu.edu

University of Michigan: telnet://mirlyn.Telnet.lib.umich.edu/

Latin American Studies

University of Pittsburgh (Andean countries): telnet://gate.cis.pitt.edu

Mexican History

University of Arizona: telnet://sabio.arizona.edu

University of Pittsburgh: telnet://gate.cis.pitt.edu

University of Texas: telnet://utxuts.dp.utexas.edu

Middle East Studies

University of Texas: telnet:// utxuts.dp.utexas.edu

University of Utah: tn3270://lib.utah.edu

Military History

Texas A&M: telnet://venus.tamu.edu (username vtam, application notis)

Duke University: telnet://ducatalog.lib.duke.edu

Mormon History

Brigham Young University: telnet://gateway.lib.byu.edu

Naval History

U.S. Naval Academy: telnet://library.nadn.navy.mil

Native American History

University of New Mexico: telnet://library.unm.edu

Nineteenth- and Twentieth-Century Political History

University of Georgia: telnet://gsvm2.cc.gasou.edu

Religious History

Duke University: telnet://ducatalog.lib.duke.edu

Renaissance

The Newberry Library: http://www.newberry.org

Slavery

Johns Hopkins: telnet://janus-gate.mse.jhu.edu

Slavic Studies

Pennsylvania State University: telnet://lias.psu.edu

Soviet Studies

Washington University of St. Louis Missouri: telnet://library.wustl.edu

Theology

Emory University: telnet://euclid.cc.emory.edu

Notre Dame: telnet://irishmvs.cc.nd.edu

Vatican Library: telnet://librs6k.vatlib.it

Western United States History

University of Colorado at Boulder: telnet://libraries.colorado.edu

Yale University: telnet://umpg.ycc.yale.edu 6520

University of Utah (Salt Lake) telnet://lib.utah.edu

ARCHIVES

In addition to libraries that house special collections, there are many archives devoted to specific areas, and many of these archives now have on-line catalogs and informational sites.

Archives and Archivists

http://miavx1.muohio.edu/~harlanjb/personal/projects/archives/

Truth in advertising, this site connects visitors to hundreds of on-line archives and archival exhibits and to a wealth of articles and resources for archivists. One can read the success and failure stories of archivists who are struggling to avoid a crash on the information superhighway or jump to hundreds of public, private, and commercial archives.

Beaton Institute Archives

http://eagle.uccb.ns.ca/beaton/beaton.html

This rich graphical project makes the holdings of the Beaton Institute Archives for Cape Breton history accessible on-line and celebrates Cape Breton.

Black Film Archive

http://www.indiana.edu/~bfca/index.html

This archive located at Indiana University centers on films by and about African-Americans.

Canadian Institute for Historical Microreprographics (CIHM)

http://www.nlc-bnc.ca/cihm/

This site locates, microfilms, and makes available early Canadian materials. A searchable index is provided.

Historical Archives of the European Communities

http://wwwarc.iue.it/

This page is an entry point to European archives.

Historical Text Archive

http://www.msstate.edu/Archives/History/index.html

This is an archive maintained by Mississippi State University. It has links to many sites all around the world, divided by country or continent and then by subject.

University of Wollongong Archives

http://www.uow.edu.au/library/archives.htm

A large collection dedicated to labor history.

MUSEUMS

Many of the world's finest museums now have Internet sites that feature information about historical collections, special on-line exhibits, research opportunities, and other details. The museums below all have collections that may be of interest to readers of *The History Highway*.

African-American National Museum Project

http://www.si.edu/resource/research/resmus/rai.htm

American Financial History Museum

http://www.netresource.com/mafh/

Ariadne's Hellenic-Greek Civilization Page

http://www.greekcivil.ariadne-t.gr/default.html

This site provides access to more than two hundred Greek museums.

Australian National Museum

http://www.nma.gov.au

Buffalo Bill Historical Center

http://wave.park.wy.us/bbhc/main.html

Canadian Museum of Civilization

http://www.cmcc.muse.digital.ca/cmc/cmceng/welcmeng.html

Chrysler Museum
http://www.whro.org/cl/cmhh/

Colonial Williamsburg
http://www.history.org/

Egyptian Museums—A Guide
http://www.idsc.gov.eg/culture/mus.htm

Eiteljorg Museum of Native American Art and History
http://www.otisnet.com/eiteljorg

Freud Museum of London
http://www.nltl.columbia.edu/students/DBS/freud/index.html

Greenfield Village—The Henry Ford Museum
http://hfm.umd.umich.edu/

Heritage Map Museum
http://www.carto.com/

Historical Museum of Crete
http://www.knossos.gr/~hmuseum/index.html

History of Science Museum (Oxford)
http://info.ox.ac.uk/departments/hooke/

Hunterian Museum (Glasgow)
http://www.gla.ac.uk/Museum/

The Louvre (France)
http://mistral.culture.fr/louvre/

The Metropolitan Museum of Art
http://www.metmuseum.org/

Michigan Historical Museum System
http://www.sos.state.mi.us/history/history.html

Musée de la Civilisation (Quebec, Canada)
http://www.mcq.org/

Museum of Antiquities
http://www.ncl.ac.uk/~nantiq/

Museum of the City of New York
http://www.tampatrib.com/mosi/

Museum of the City of San Francisco
http://www.slip.net/~dfowler/1906/museum.html

Museum of the Regiments (Canada)
http://www.lexicom.ab.ca:80/~regiments/

Museum of Slavery
http://squash.la.psu.edu/plarson/smuseum/homepage.html

National Air and Space Museum
http://www.si.edu/resource/research/resmus/rnasm.htm

National Building Museum
http://www.nbm.org/

National Museum of American History
http://www.si.edu/organiza/museums/nmah/homepage/nmah.htm

National Museum of the American Indian
http://www.si.edu/resource/research/resmus/ramind.htm

National Museums of Scotland
http://www.nms.ac.uk

National Palace Museum (Taiwan)
http://www.npm.gov.tw/

National Postal Museum
http://www.si.edu/resource/research/resmus/rpost.htm

Shiloh Museum of Ozark History
http://www.uark.edu/ALADDIN/shiloh

The Simon Wiesenthal Center
http://www.wiesenthal.com

Singapore On-Line Museum of Art and History
http://www.ncb.gov.sg/nhb/museum.html

Smithsonian Institution Home Page
http://www.si.edu/

Snoqualmie Valley Historical Museum
http://www.bush.edu/wpages/snoq.html

United States Holocaust Memorial Museum
http://www.ushmm.org/

Wagga Wagga (Australian) Historical Museum
http://www.canb.auug.org.au/~stmcdona/museum.html

The White House
http://www.whitehouse.gov/WH/Tours/White_House/Welcome.html

Woodrow Wilson House
http://sunsite.unc.edu/lia/president/pressites/wilson/WilsonH-brochure
.html

AN ON-LINE REFERENCE DESK

American Universities
http://www.clas.ufl.edu/CLAS/american-universities.html

This site contains a major list of links to on-line universities and colleges in the United States.

Bartlett's Familiar Quotations

http://www.cc.columbia.edu/acis/bartleby/bartlett/index.html

Biblical Names Dictionary

http://www.goshen.net/hbn/

This site provides a list of Biblical names and their meanings.

C-Net's Shareware

http://www.shareware.com/

This is a search engine that lists over 130,000 shareware computer programs and connects to sites where they can be downloaded.

CIA World Factbook

http://www.odci.gov/cia/publications/95fact/index.html

This is an excellent source for getting quick information for all the countries in the world. Each country has a listing of current populations, demographics, literacy rates, government officials, and economic information.

Computer Dictionary

http://wombat.doc.ic.ac.uk/foldoc/contents.html

The Computer Dictionary is an on-line, searchable index of common computer terms.

Dictionary of Acronyms

gopher://info.mcc.ac.uk:70/11/miscellany/acronyms

Encyclopaedia Britannica On-Line

http://www.eb.com/

There is a fee to use this site.

ENews: The Electronic Newsstand

http://www.enews.com/

This site allows you to search for articles and features from thousands of magazines and newspapers.

FAQ Search Engine

http://www.cs.ruu.nl/cgi-bin/faqwais

The FAQ Search Engine permits users to search a large database of newsgroup Frequently Asked Questions (FAQs).

Find-A-Grave

http://www.orci.com/personal/jim/index.html

This site allows you to locate the graves of many famous figures. The database is organized by last name and geographic location. Pictures of some of the graves are included.

Foreign Language Dictionaries

http://www.uiuc.edu/refs/dict.top.html

Free Internet Encyclopedia

http://www.cs.uh.edu/~clifton/encyclopedia.html

Unlike your traditional encyclopedia which provides information, this site is an indexed set of links to sites on hundreds of different topics.

History Departments Around the World

http://web.gmu.edu/departments/history/research/depts.html

This is an alphabetical listing of links to history department home pages in the United States and other countries.

InfoMine

http://lib-www.ucr.edu/

InfoMine is a large database of links to Internet sites divided thematically. This search engine also accesses all available on-line government publications.

Intellectual Property Law Hotlinks

http://w3.gwis.com/~sarbar/index.html

Intellectual Property Law Hotlinks connects visitors to a number of sites on intellectual property issues, including patents, trademarks, copyrights, and other links.

Intellectual Property Rights

http://www.lightlink.com/bbm/index.html

Presented by Barnard, Brown, and Michaels, a New York intellectual property firm, this site provides legal information concerning patents, trademarks, and copyrights. The site also provides on-line estimates of the legal fees for various services.

Librarians' Guide to Internet Information Sources

http://www.sau.edu/CWIS/internet/wild/index.htm

Created by St. Ambrose University, the Librarians' Guide to Internet Information Sources is an excellent gateway to resources on the Net which will help or interest librarians. It includes links to "hot paper topics," national and international newspapers, search engines, sites for librarians, and job-hunting guides.

MLA-Style Citation of Electronic Sources

http://www.cas.usf.edu/english/walker/mla.html

NYNEX Internet Yellow Pages

http://s16.bigyellow.com/

This site contains national telephone listings for businesses.

Oxford English Dictionary On-Line

http://www.oed.com/dicts.html

There is a fee to use this site.

Pathfinder's NewsNow

http://pathfinder.com/@@jKOZcQQA1xx1KXmo/welcome

Pathfinder's NewsNow is a searchable database of news articles as well as articles from such popular magazines as *Time, Life, People,* and *Money.*

Statistical Abstracts of the United States

http://wwww.census.gov/stat_abstract/

This is an excellent source for almost any sort of statistical information: demographics, income, dates, employment, health information, industrial production statistics, and government financial information.

Strunk's *Elements of Style*

http://www.columbia.edu/acis/bartleby/strunk/index.html

Switchboard

http://www.switchboard.com/

Switchboard is a search engine that is ideal for locating the addresses and phone numbers of more 90 million people. The site also lists e-mail addresses for registered users.

Thesaurus On-Line

gopher://odie.niaid.nih.gov/77/.thesaurus/index

Turabian-Style Citation Guide for Internet Sources

http://www.kaiwan.com/~lucknow/horus/etexts/citenet.html

United States Bureau of the Census Server

http://tiger.census.gov/cgi-bin/gazetteer

This is a server that provides census data on all incorporated municipalities in the United States. Maps provided, and this database is searchable.

United States Government Copyright Information and Registration

gopher://marvel.loc.gov [**From the menu select: Copyright**]

This site explains how to file a copyright, what can be copyrighted, the terms of copyright, and much related information. You can also request a copyright registration form from this site.

United States Telephone Area Codes

gopher://odie.niaid.nih.gov/77/deskref/.areacode/index

Key in the city and state to this searchable database, it will provide the area code.

United States Zipcodes

http://www.cedar.buffalo.edu/adserv.html

Key in the street name and town, and this site will give you a list of probable zip codes.

U.S. News Online

http://www.usnews.com/usnews/

This site does searches of *U.S. News* for specific titles and subjects of news stories.

Virtual Library

http://www.albany.edu/library/newlib/index.html

A huge variety of services is provided by this virtual library. Quick references, subject and library catalogs, electronic publications, career information, and fee-based services are all provided, linked, or described.

Virtual Reference Desk

http://thorplus.lib.purdue.edu/reference/index.html

This Purdue University site lists dictionaries, thesauruses, zip code directories, and other reference works of use to historians and other scholars.

Webster's Dictionary

http://c.gp.cs.cmu.edu:5103/prog/webster

GENERAL WORLD WIDE WEB SEARCH ENGINES FOR THE INTERNET

One of the most popular and useful features of the Internet is the search engine. Search engines greatly simplify the process of finding and accessing information on the Internet. In many ways the phenomenal growth of the World Wide Web is due to the creation of commercial search engines which make finding specific names and places on the Internet faster and easier. There are now dozens of such programs that search the Internet in a variety of ways, providing lists of sites relevant to one's query. These search engines are also continuing to evolve, becoming faster, more powerful, and easier to use. They are now one of the most valuable tools for finding historical information and other data on the Internet.

There are still some drawbacks to search engines, however. One of the main problems is that they make no judgments on the usefulness of information. If you use a general search engine such as Yahoo to find sites related to the American Civil War and just type the words "Civil War" into the query box, you will be given more than ten thousand entries to examine. Not only would this be overwhelming, but in many cases the majority of the links would not be pertinent to your search. You would find links for everything from the latest news on the Bosnian Civil War to a paper on General Ulysses S. Grant by a sixth-grader in Boston. Within these thousands of links would lie a wealth of useful information, but sifting through the unwanted materials could be a draining and frustrating task.

A couple of useful hints make searching on the Internet quicker, easier, and more useful. First, always make your search as specific as possible. When the search engine requests key words or terms, give clear and precise words, since it is this information that the engine will compare with all the entries in its database for matches. For example, if you are looking for an on-line copy of Mark Twain's *Life on the Mississippi,* a good starting point would be typing the words "*Life on the Mississippi*" and "Mark Twain" in the query box. This would give you a smaller number of results than just typing in "Mark Twain" or "Life on the Mississippi."

Many search engines will also ask how many results you want returned, and limiting this number is an excellent way to speed searches. Often the first hundred results will contain a link to the information that you are looking for. Of course, if the first hundred returns are not helpful, you can always run the search again with higher limits.

Finally, remember that each search engine will yield slightly different results. If you do not find what you are after on the first try, use another engine. If you want the broadest possible search, use each of the major search engines listed below. This list does not cover all of them, but it does give information on the largest and most popular. Links to dozens of others can be found at:

All-In-One Search Page (http://www.albany.net/allinone/).

AltaVista

http://www.altavista.com/

This is one of the most powerful search engines currently available. AltaVista allows users to search both the World Wide Web and Usenet groups, and it will return results in a standard, compact, or detailed format.

Dejanews

http://www.dejanews.com/

Billed as the "premier usenet search utility," Dejanews allows the user to search the archives of Usenet groups and current lists.

GNN

http://nearnet.gnn.com/gnn/index.html

GNN, the Global Network Navigator, provides a large subject index that can be searched by key word or key phrase.

HotBot

http://www.hotbot.com/

This is a new search engine that enables the user to search the Web by key word, key phrase, person, or URL.

Lycos

http://lycos.cs.cmu.edu/

Lycos is a powerful search engine which allows users to search either a subject index or the complete database by key words.

Magellan Internet Guide

http://www.mckinley.com/

This increasingly popular search engine indexes, rates and reviews Web sites.

Webcrawler

http://www.webcrawler.com

Webcrawler is a standard search engine that offers quick and easy results for Web searches.

Yahoo!

http://www.yahoo.com/

Yahoo! is one of the largest databases. It provides an index of sites arranged thematically and allows key word or key phrase searches.

Glossary

Alias: A name used in place of a "real" name. Aliases are often shorter or more clever than a person's real name.

ASCII: The American Standard Code for Information Interchange. This is a way of formatting data so that it can be read by any program, whether DOS, Windows, or Mac.

BBS: Bulletin Board System. This term usually refers to small dial-up systems that local users can call directly.

Browser: A program used to access the World Wide Web. The most popular browsers—Netscape and Mosaic—allow users to interact audiovisually with the World Wide Web.

Client: A synonym for Web browser or browser.

Document: On the World Wide Web, a document can be either a file or a set of files which can be accessed with a Web browser.

Domain Name System (DNS): DNS is the system that locates addresses on the World Wide Web. When a DNS error message is given by a browser, it means the address it is looking for cannot be found.

Download: The process of getting a file or files from a remote computer; that is, a computer other than the one on your desk or local area network.

Electronic Mail (e-mail): Sending typed messages and attachments through an electronic mail network.

FAQ: Frequently Asked Questions. A FAQ is a document that contains answers to the most frequently asked questions about a given topic.

File: A collection of data stored on a disk or other storage device under a certain name.

File Transfer Protocol (FTP): A tool for moving files from another computer site to your local service provider's computer, from which it can be downloaded.

Flame: The practice of sending negative or insulting e-mail.

GIF: Graphic Interchange Format. A set of standards for compressing graphic files so that they occupy less space in a computer's memory or on a storage device. GIF was developed by CompuServe and Unisys.

Gopher: An older method of navigating the Internet developed at the University of Minnesota (where the mascot is the Golden Gopher). It displays information and links to documents, but is not graphics-based and is more difficult to use than the World Wide Web. Gopher is rapidly being replaced by the World Wide Web.

H-Net: The Humanities Network, or Humanities On-Line Initiative. H-Net is an organization dedicated to exploiting the potential of electronic media for history. It is supported by the National Endowment for the Humanities, the University of Illinois–Chicago, and Michigan State University. H-Net sponsors discussion lists, Web sites, book reviews, conferences, and other activities.

Hits: This is Internet slang for both the number of times a site is accessed by a user and the number of sites found when using any Web search engine.

Home Page: A home page is the designated beginning point for accessing a World Wide Web site.

HTML: Hypertext Markup Language. The computer language used to construct documents on the World Wide Web. Most home pages are written in HTML.

HTTP: Hypertext Transfer Protocol. A method of coding information that enables different computers running different software to communicate information. It permits the transfer of text, sounds, images, and other data.

Hypermedia: Computer-generated displays that combine text, images, and sound.

Hyptertext: Data that provides links to other data allowing one to move from one resource to another.

Icon: A graphic image that is used to represent (and usually activate) a file or program.

Internet: The worldwide network of computers that is linked together using the Internet Protocol, TCP/IP.

Java: A new programming language developed by Sun Microsystems that allows programmers to create interactive applications that can be run within Web browsers.

JPEG: Joint Photographic Experts Group. This is now the standard format for compressing graphic files so that they occupy less space in a computer's memory or on a storage device.

Link: A connection point, which might take you from one document to another or from one information provider to another.

Listserv: A computer that serves a discussion group by processing, distributing, and storing messages and files for all members of the list.

Local Area Network (LAN): A group of computers connected together by cable or some other means so that they can share common resources.

Log in: The process of gaining access to a remote computer system or network by typing one's login name and password.

Login name: The name you use for security purposes to gain access to a network or computer system.

MPEG: Moving Pictures Expert Group. The standard for compressing video images so that they occupy less space in a computer's memory or on a storage device.

Netiquette: Etiquette for the Internet.

Network: A group of interconnected computers.

Page: Page can refer either to a single screen of information on a Web site or to all of the information on a particular site.

RAM: Random Access Memory. RAM is the memory that your computer uses to temporarily store and manipulate information. RAM does not hold information after your computer is turned off.

Service Provider: Any organization that provides connections to the Internet.

SLIP/PPP Serial Line Internet Protocol/Point to Point Protocol: A connection that enables a home computer to receive TCP/IP addresses. To work with the World Wide Web from home via a modem, a SLIP or PPP connection is necessary.

TCP/IP Transfer Control Protocol/Internet Protocol: Essentially this is the most basic language on the Internet. The rules of TCP/IP govern the sending of packets of data between computers on the Internet, and they allow for the transmission of other protocols on the Internet, such as http and FTP.

Telnet: An Internet protocol that enables you to log on to a remote computer.

UNIX: Like DOS or Windows, UNIX is an operating system run by most of the computers that provide access to the Internet.

URL: Uniform Resource Locator. The address for an Internet site.

USENET: A network of newsgroups dedicated to thousands of different topics.

Web Browser: A program used to access the World Wide Web. The most popular browsers—Netscape and Mosaic—allow users to interact audiovisually with the World Wide Web.

Winsock: A program that runs in the background on a Windows-based personal computer, allowing you to make a SLIP/PPP connection to the Internet and to use the TCP/IP protocols.

World Wide Web (WWW): An Internet service that enables you to connect to all of the hypermedia documents on the Internet. The Web is like a network within the Internet.

Suggestions for Further Reading

The number of introductory and technical guides to Internet software and hardware seems to be expanding nearly as fast as the Internet itself. Excellent books are now produced for most software programs before the programs ever reach the market. Thus, anyone searching for a more in-depth discussion of the themes covered in chapter 1 will have no trouble finding a good manual. The guides suggested below include many of the best and most popular books that are presently available.

GENERAL GUIDES TO THE INTERNET AND THE WORLD WIDE WEB

Cady, Glee Harrah, and McGregor, Pat. *Mastering the Internet.* San Francisco: Sybex, 1995. *Mastering the Internet* is a good general guide that discusses the Internet and all its tools in great detail. The technical details are made clearer through the use of many illustrations, and it also includes a cd-rom with all the software you need to get started. Both the book and the cd-rom, however, stress the Netcruiser browser, rather than Netscape.

December, John, and Randall, Neil. *The World Wide Web Unleashed.* Indianapolis: Sams Publishing, 1996. *The World Wide Web Unleashed* is an excellent comprehensive guide to the Web. It covers every aspect of the WWW from using and selecting a browser to creating your own Web site, and it is illustrated with many helpful images. The book is also accompanied by a cd-rom that includes the software needed to access the Web and to perform advanced tasks such as writing hypertext pages. Net novices may find it a bit too detailed, but users who have a grasp on Internet use would find it a first-rate general guide.

Eager, Bill. *Using the World Wide Web.* Indianapolis: Que, 1996. *Using the World Wide Web* is very good detailed guide to every aspect of the World Wide Web. It provides a high degree of technical detail, discusses many advanced features, and covers all of the latest software programs. It also comes with a cd-rom that includes all the programs you will need to access the World Wide Web, including Netscape, an html publisher, and many others. Those who are completely new to the Web might want to consider another book, however, since Eager assumes a lot of knowledge.

Gilster, Paul. *The New Internet Navigator.* New York: John Wiley & Sons, 1995. *The New Internet Navigator* is the best general guide to the Internet. It covers nearly every conceivable aspect of the Internet in easy-to-understand detail, and Paul Gilster writes with a literary eloquence that makes his books enjoyable and informative. This is an excellent choice for any Internet traveler.

Levine, John R., and Young, Margaret Levine. *The Internet for Dummies.* Foster City, CA: IDG, 1995. *The Internet for Dummies* is an excellent general introduction to the Internet. Like all books in the "for Dummies" series, it is written in simple, straightforward language and is richly illustrated with helpful pictures and graphs. *The Internet for Dummies* does not provide much technical detail or great depth, but it provides clear instructions for the basic Internet tools such as e-mail, FTP, Telnet, and Netscape. It is a good choice for Internet beginners.

———. *More Internet for Dummies.* Foster City, CA: IDG, 1996. *More Internet for Dummies* goes several steps beyond *The Internet for Dummies.* It provides additional technical information and goes into the more advanced features of Internet software packages. *More Internet for Dummies* also discusses the latest versions of Netscape and other programs, explaining important changes and new features.

Seiter, Charles. *Internet for Macs for Dummies.* Foster City, CA: IDG,

1994. Although it is now somewhat dated, *Internet for Macs for Dummies* contains clear discussions of essential Internet tools such as FTP, e-mail, and Web browsing. The book does not address recent versions of Netscape, Eudora, and other important packages, but beginning Mac explorers of the Internet may still find it helpful.

Stauffer, Todd. *Using the Internet with Your Mac.* Indianapolis: Que, 1995. *Using the Internet with Your Mac* is a good introduction to the Internet software available for the Macintosh. It discusses all of the basic Internet tools in simple but informative prose. The guide does not contain great detail, but beginning users would find it useful.

Wagner, Ronald L., and Englemann, Eric. *The McGraw-Hill Internet Training Manual.* New York: McGraw-Hill, 1996. *The McGraw-Hill Internet Training Manual* is an excellent introduction to the Internet. It takes readers through all of the basic tools needed to use the Internet, and it has excellent full-color illustrations to accompany the text. This is a good choice for those with little or no experience navigating the Net, but it does not contain enough detail to suit more advanced users.

NETSCAPE

Brown, Mark. *Using Netscape 2.* Indianapolis: Que, 1995. *Using Netscape 2* is a complete guide to all of Netscape's features. The guide is also well-illustrated and contains a cd-rom with Netscape and many supporting programs. This guide provides more detail and technical information than a beginning user needs or wants.

Hoffman, Paul. *Netscape and the World Wide Web for Dummies.* Foster City, CA: IDG, 1996. *Netscape and the World Wide Web for Dummies* is a good introduction for beginning Netscape users. It does not discuss many advanced features, but those who feel comfortable with the "for Dummies" series or who only want a simple guide to Netscape will like this book.

James, Phil. *Official Netscape Navigator 2.0 Book.* Research Triangle Park, NC: Netscape Press, 1996. The *Official Netscape Navigator 2.0 Book* is an excellent guide to all of the features of Netscape 2.0, and since it is produced by the people who created the software, it contains many helpful insider's tips. The book is very well illustrated and is packaged along with a cd-rom including Netscape 2.0 and several programs that can run with it. It is appropriate for users of all levels.

NETIQUETTE AND LEGAL ISSUES

Cavazos, Edward A., and Morin, Govino. *Cyberspace and the Law.* Cambridge: MIT Press, 1995. *Cyberspace and the Law* explores many of the thorniest issues associated with the Internet, from privacy to intellectual property, from slander and libel to on-line pornography. Written for a lay audience, it is clear and insightful enough to interest anyone concerned with the laws and rules governing the Net.

Mandel, Thomas, and Gerard Van der Leun. *Rules of the Net.* New York: Hyperion, 1996. *Rules of the Net* is an excellent account of Netiquette and the laws regulating the Net. It covers topics ranging from e-mail style to intellectual property and provides the most up-to-date treatment of the subjects.

Smedinghoff, Thomas J. *On-Line Law: The SPA's Legal Guide to Doing Business on the Internet.* Reading, MA: Addison Wesley, 1996. *On-Line Law* is a more than a guide to doing business on the Internet. It is an up-to-date and clearly written account of all the legal and security issues affecting the Net. Readers of *The History Highway* will find the sections on intellectual property and security particularly interesting.

HTML AND WEB PAGE CREATION

Lawrence, David, and Mark, Dave. *Learn HTML on the Macintosh.* Reading, MA: Addison Wesley, 1996. *Learn HTML on the Macintosh* is the best introduction to creating Web pages on the Macintosh. It covers the basics of HTML code in clear, simple language. Mac users who want to begin putting their own Web sites on-line would profit from this book.

Stauffer, Todd. *HTML by Example*. Indianapolis: Que, 1996. *HTML by Example* is an excellent beginners' guide to writing pages for the World Wide Web. The book is richly illustrated with hundreds of examples, and it comes with a cd-rom that includes software that makes creating Web pages quick and simple. This is a very good book for beginners.

Tittel, Ed, and James, Steve. *HTML for Dummies*. Foster City, CA: IDG, 1995. *HTML for Dummies* is a good introduction to creating World Wide Web sites. The book covers all the basics you need to know to get your own site on-line. It does not cover many advanced features, but it is a clear guide for beginners.

EDUCATION AND THE INTERNET

Greenstein, Daniel. *A Historian's Guide to Computing*. Oxford: Oxford University Press, 1994. The *Historian's Guide to Computing* focuses almost exclusively on the use of databases and word processors in historical research. There is no mention of the World Wide Web and very little on Internet tools such as e-mail, Telnet, and FTP. For scholars who would like to venture into quantitative or statistical research, however, this remains the best introduction.

Powell, Thomas, et al. *The Educator's Internet Yellow Pages—A Web Surfer Book*. Upper Saddle River, NJ: Prentice Hall, 1996. *The Educator's Internet Yellow Pages* is a guide to the World Wide Web for K–12 teachers. It contains a basic introduction to the Internet and lists thirty to fifty sites for subjects from biology to Spanish. There are few resources dealing specifically with history, but the book contains good references to general teaching issues, course construction suggestions, and K–12 forums.

Williams, B. *The Internet for Teachers*. Foster City, CA: IDG, 1995. *The Internet for Teachers* is a basic introduction to the Internet for K–12 teachers. It contains little on the World Wide Web, however, and the disk included with the book contains software that is now slightly outdated. A new edition is needed.

Index

Entries in *italics* are Internet sites.

Dennis A. Trinkle is the co-founder and co-editor of *History Reviews On-Line*, the first on-line historical journal devoted to scholarly book reviews [http://www.uc.edu/www/history/reviews.htmlx], and a Taft Doctoral Fellow in History at the University of Cincinnati. He is a member of the editorial board of *H-France* and is the developer and editor of the *H-France* World Wide Web and Gopher Sites. He is the co-chair of the Cincinnati Symposium on Computers and the Future of History, and he has written articles on the practice of history in the electronic age for the *Organization of American Historians Newsletter*, the *Organization of American Historians Council of Chairs Newsletter*, and *University Currents*. Dennis Trinkle contributed to every section of the book.

Dorothy Auchter is a reference librarian at Wright State University. She holds master's degrees in both history and library science. She has served as a reference librarian in several major universities, including Indiana University and the Kinsey Institute. Her publication credits include a quarterly column in *History Reviews On-Line*, as well as contributions to the professional library journals *Choice* and *Journal of Academic Librarianship*. She is a member of the American Library Association and serves as the ALA's history specialist, evaluating and recommending reference books for special ALA recognition. Dorothy Auchter contributed to every section of chapter 2.

Scott A. Merriman teaches American history at Northern Kentucky University and the University of Cincinnati. He is an assistant editor for *History Reviews On-Line* and has contributed to the *Historical*

Encyclopedia of World Slavery and *American National Biography.* He has reviewed books for *The Historian, Southern Historian,* and *Civil War History.* Professor Merriman has also written numerous articles on the Espionage and Sedition Act trials in Ohio and Kentucky and on the anti-German hysteria during World War I. Scott Merriman contributed to every section of chapter 2.

Todd E. Larson is a Graduate Research Assistant at the National Center for Supercomputing Applications (NCSA) and a doctoral candidate in modern British history at the University of Illinois, Urbana-Champaign. At present he is overseeing the development of the Beckman Institute's Project RiverWebTM—a World Wide Web project that will present a history and culture of the Mississippi River. He has also served as the graduate research assistant responsible for implementing computer-related resources for history undergraduates, graduates, and faculty at the University of Illinois. Along with Dennis Trinkle, he is co-founder and co-editor of *History Reviews On-Line.* He has also written a number of articles and pamphlets on the future of history in the computer age. Todd Larson contributed to the sections on electronic journals, general history sites, and search engines.